T0193952

7 SECRETS from the Divorce Whisperer

SAVING YOURSELF, YOUR MONEY, AND
YOUR CHILDREN DURING DIVORCE

MARTA J. PAPA, J.D.

BALBOA.
PRESS
A DIVISION OF HAY HOUSE

Balboa Press books may be ordered through booksellers or by contacting:

Balboa Press
A Division of Hay House
1663 Liberty Drive
Bloomington, IN 47403
www.balboapress.com
1 (877) 407-4847

Print information available on the last page.

ISBN: 978-1-9822-2885-9 (sc)
ISBN: 978-1-9822-2886-6 (hc)
ISBN: 978-1-9822-2919-1 (e)

Library of Congress Control Number: 2019906531

Balboa Press rev. date: 07/11/2019

Contents

To every soul facing the crisis of divorce, may this
book be your lifeline to a better future.

To my daughter, Jessica, who bravely weathered the storm of my
own divorce from her father when she was only eleven years old.

To Tim Galvin, MSW, my mentor and instructor at
the Menninger Institute, who *never let me quit.*

Preface

In the lowest moments of a teetering marriage, when the bonds are fraying or there has been betrayal, deception, violence, or stress beyond endurance, the idea of divorce surfaces. With it comes waves of anger, frustration, fear, and confusion. This is when real help is needed. What people in this fragile state need most is knowledgeable help in sorting through their feelings, clarifying their thoughts, and preparing themselves for the big choices ahead. They need a lifeline to a better future.

7 Secrets from the Divorce Whisperer: How to Save Yourself, Your Money, and Your Children During Divorce, is that lifeline. As a practicing divorce lawyer for thirty years and a divorcee myself, I have a profound empathy for people caught in this emotional maelstrom. When my own marriage was falling apart, I prowled the aisles of bookstores, searching for a book that would be compassionate, knowledgeable, uplifting, and accessible all at the same time. A book I could trust, consult, and reread in solitude to help me cut through the mental fog of emotion and think my way forward. Such a book, I knew, would be nourishment for my brain and tonic for my soul. I wanted clarity, but I also wanted inspiration and hope.

I found many books at the time, but not a single one brought all these elements together in the way I sought. I decided then that I would write the book about divorce that was missing from the shelves. *This* book is the one I needed and could not find. *This* book is the one I want all my clients to read before or in the wake of our first meeting. *This* book is written for them and for everyone facing the life crisis that no one is ever really prepared to face.

The first chapter tackles a core question seldom addressed. I believe every person contemplating the upending of life as they know it should first undertake an emotional inventory of self and marriage, getting at the real roots of unhappiness. How else to fit the right tool to the problem? It is immeasurably helpful to consider these questions honestly as a prelude. Your therapist (I always encourage clients to seek counseling) and your lawyer will thank you. This essential step of self-clarification, vital to a successful outcome, is often skipped; it's too tempting to ride the tidal wave of anger instead. But is the marriage really to blame for one's unhappiness? Is divorce really the answer?

This book provides the knowledge and framework to prepare oneself for the decisions ahead. An entire chapter is devoted to domestic violence. Two chapters address how the divorce affects children, both before and after the actual dissolution of marriage, and what parents can do to mitigate the damage. There are chapters on different types of divorce, and on mediation, the smartest option for dissolving most marriages. *7 Secrets from the Divorce Whisperer* is meant to guide every soul who is going through the life-altering process of divorce.

Marriage is tough. Divorce, even tougher. Everybody needs help navigating the legal morass, to say nothing of the stress and heartbreak. This book is that compassionate friend who helps you find the strength, clarity, and resolve you thought you'd lost forever; the friend who gives you the conviction that you can be the architect of your best possible future.

HOW I BECAME "THE DIVORCE WHISPERER"

The story behind how I earned the moniker "The Divorce Whisperer" started with losing my voice for about one year. As you can imagine, this was not an ideal condition for a single, self-supporting divorcee who relies on her voice to make a living.

I was diagnosed with two vocal cord tumors that had to be removed surgically if I ever wanted to speak again. I was told that, even with surgery, I had a fifty-fifty chance of being mute for the rest of my life. I wouldn't know if I would regain my voice until six to nine months after the surgery. My doctor said that if my vocal cords repaired themselves, my voice would come back as a whisper. However, my doctor suggested I get my affairs in order before the surgery.

Following his advice, I referred all my clients to other lawyers and mediators. A few refused to leave. I found it strange that clients would put their divorce on hold based on my medical condition. But, nevertheless, they refused to change lawyers. The ones who stayed with me would call every month to see if I'd gotten my voice back yet; my secretary would give them the bad news each day that I was still mute. Then one morning, about six months later, I woke up and could whisper.

That fateful morning when I could finally bring my vocal chords together to make sounds, the phone rang in the office. I heard my secretary answer that, yes, I could whisper, as she proceeded to set up an appointment for later that week. When I inquired who had called, I was shocked. It was a particularly difficult couple that I had worked with before the surgery. They were difficult because the wife had had an affair, and the husband wanted to punish and shame her for it. When we worked on dividing property, every time he asked for a particular asset and she agreed he could take it, he launched into a verbal attack, telling his wife, "You'd better give that to me, you goddamn effing whore!"

Trying to stay calm and collected, I pointed out that this tactic was not helping him because every time he called her this derogatory term, his wife would take back her offer. I worked with him, offering physical cues that he was about to launch into his verbal attack, to no avail.

When they came in to resume their mediation, I greeted them in a whisper, so they whispered back. The constant whispering caused us all to lean together to hear each other. The first time he requested a property asset, his wife agreed. But as soon as she agreed, he whispered the same derogatory retort: "You'd better give that to me, you goddamn effing whore!"

This time, however, she didn't respond or retract her offer as before because it was said in a whisper. Husband never called her those names again; the words clearly lost their impact when whispered. We settled all remaining issues in their divorce in a mere two hours.

As I walked them to the door, they whispered goodbye and thanked me. I closed the door, turned to my secretary, and said, "How did that happen?"

She replied, "You whispered them to an agreement!"

I didn't think much more about the incident until one day I told the story to a group of friends when we were out for lunch. One friend leaned back in her chair laughing and said, "Oh my gosh! You're the divorce whisperer!" I smiled and the name stuck.

Meaning of the Dandelion Flower

You will find pictures of a dandelion flower throughout this book. I have included these images because the dandelion has come to symbolize surviving adversity and rising about such difficulties. This is my wish for all who read this book. Every time you see a dandelion, let it serve as a reminder that you will survive the storm of divorce and eventually thrive as a result of all you learn about yourself during the divorce process.

The First Secret

CONSIDERING DIVORCE?

Ask yourself some crucial questions before taking action.

After over thirty years of guiding unhappy couples through the divorce process, here is what I know:

1. You deserve to be happy.
2. You deserve to lead a fulfilling and peaceful life, free of constant conflict.
3. You deserve to be the creator of your future, rather than a prisoner of someone else's control.
4. You deserve a life free of fear for your own physical safety and that of your children.
5. You deserve a life free of constant worry that the stability of your family life is threatened by the unreliability of teamwork in your marriage.
6. You deserve to exercise your power to protect yourself and your children from abuse, instability, and conflict.
7. You deserve respect and you should be the first and most constant source of this, in your thoughts, decisions, and actions regarding your own life.
8. You deserve respect from the other significant people in your life.

9. You deserve an abundant life with the ability to make your own choices about money: how to earn it, how to spend it, and how to make it work for your long-term needs.

10. You deserve a place to live where you are safe, content, in control of your surroundings, and able to lock the door to keep out anyone or anything that does not bring you peace. You deserve your own sanctuary.

Sound like the kind of life you want to live? Well, you can. The purpose of this book is to show you how. Right now, there might be a lot of things standing between you and that kind of safe, peaceful, and affirming life. This book gives you the tools you need to think clearly and start taking steps toward that better life. As you will see, asking yourself the *right* questions is the best place to start. And asking yourself the *right* questions at every stage thereafter is the way to move forward. I am bringing all my professional experience to the cause of helping you ask the right questions and avoid a multitude of pitfalls that could deepen your unhappiness and cause you a lot of wasted time and money.

The power to create the life you want may involve declaring freedom from your spouse—or *not*. As you can imagine, this is an extremely important question, and you *must take the time you need* to answer it accurately for yourself. My goal is to help guide you through a step-by-step process to answer the question of whether to stay or leave and the ones that naturally follow from it, so you are empowered with the knowledge you need to create the life you want.

When I meet with potential clients, I tell them that if they want me to work with them, they *must* answer the list of crucial questions I send home with them. If they decide to hire me, they must bring the questions to our next meeting. I have found that this information makes a tremendous difference in getting my clients what they want during divorce. Clients who have thoroughly considered these questions are far more focused and centered.

Asking yourself the right questions starts the process that leads to sound decision making and an energizing sense of empowerment in shaping your future. If you thoughtfully answer the questions in this book, you will find a roadmap to follow as you move forward, and the journey will bring you to the destination that's been waiting for you all along.

Below I have set out my list of crucial questions that you need to answer right now. Your honest responses are critical to making sure that you focus on the real cause of your problems. For example, if you have scurvy and someone advises you to take iron tablets, you're not going to solve your problem. Even though appropriate amounts of iron are good for you, you need vitamin C to cure scurvy. In the same way, finding the correct cause of your unhappiness is crucial in resolving your issue.

You are about to walk through the portal toward a new life. Are you ready?

THE CRUCIAL QUESTIONS

1. What kind of life do you need to live to be happy?
2. What would that life look like? Draw a picture of it, putting in all the essential elements necessary for it to be your ideal life.
3. In what ways are you already living this life?
4. In what ways are you not living it?
5. Why not?
6. What needs to change so you can live this life?
7. Change is multifaceted. What changes do you need to make in how you think and act? What changes in attitude and actions do you believe need to come from someone other than yourself in order to move closer to the life you envisioned in question number 2?
8. If you could magically leap right now into your ideal future, how would your new situation affect other people in your life? Draw a picture of yourself with circles radiating outward of people who

would be affected. Note how you believe such a change would likely affect them.

9. Who do you need to consult to help you think about how you feel now and how you want to feel in the future?

10. What in your life now brings you a sense of contentment?

11. What are your current sources of conflict, fear, or stress?

12. What would need to happen to end this conflict, fear, or stress? Remember that the only actions and attitudes we really have the power to change are our own. We cannot change others. We can either ask them to voluntarily behave differently around us, or we can remove ourselves from the situation.

13. Do you feel controlled or dominated by someone or something? Name this controlling force. How does this play out in your life? Why is it happening? Make a drawing if this helps you think this through. Think about spouse, children, other relatives, job, studies, needs, and desires.

14. If your response to question thirteen includes naming a person, what kind of discussion would you need to have with this person to break the pattern? Do you believe this pattern of control and domination can be broken?

15. What needs to happen for you to take back your power?

16. How much power do you feel you have over money: making it, spending it, and deciding how to grow and preserve it for the long term?

17. If you don't control the money, who does, and why?

18. Can that system be changed? How?

19. Make a list of your greatest fears and the things you worry about the most.

20. How many of these things can you control? Not control?

21. What would have to change in your life to lessen your fears?

22. Do you see a pattern emerging regarding the source of these things you fear and worry about? What is that pattern?

23. What would need to happen for you to feel you deserve respect for yourself and from others?

24. Who in your life right now gives you respect? Do you know why? Do you feel you deserve it? Why or why not?

I'm certain you could add to this list of questions regarding your happiness, sense of control over your life, and ability to live in peace without fear. Let me encourage you to do so. This is your opportunity to examine your life and compare it to the life you want to live.

Most important, though, is that you begin to examine who is responsible for your not living the life you want.

Of course, the only person ultimately responsible for your happiness is you. Right? But there may be other factors at work, including other people, that seriously compromise your efforts to increase your happiness. If so, it is important to be able to identify such conditions and such people.

- Don't blame your spouse for conditions that are outside his or her control.
- Don't blame your spouse if you have an untreated addiction.
- Don't blame your spouse for things other people do that interfere with your goals.

On the other hand, if these questions keep leading you back to your spouse's actions, then it is time for you to acknowledge problems in that relationship and decide whether you are going to take any action to change the status quo. You must ask yourself these questions to determine whether your spouse is the origin of your biggest concerns.

If you find after clear-eyed examination of your life that your spouse is *not* the origin of your biggest concerns, then a divorce probably will not help you resolve these issues. The obvious next steps are to seek the help you need to address those concerns, whether it be through counseling, treatment, financial advice, career counseling, or something else. Your commitment and follow through will bring you the empowerment you need to improve your life. Divorce is a huge life change with many consequences and is sometimes not the right course of action. Are you in danger of sacrificing a relationship that could be repaired and improved? Are you on the verge of subjecting yourself and your children to a potentially destabilizing and emotionally draining process when you don't have to?

If, on the other hand, you find that your spouse is the cause of your greatest concerns, then a divorce should make your life better, provided you make wise and reasonable decisions throughout the process.

If you've thoroughly answered the questions posed so far and are still thinking about divorce, it's time to move on to the next level of focus. The next section includes a set of questions designed to double-check that finding that divorce is what you want.

Is divorce really the right tool for the job? You may think you've already answered that question and don't need to review it, but my experience tells me that is rarely the case. You need to look closer and know more. Get ready for the reality check!

THE REALITY CHECK: FITTING THE TOOL TO THE PROBLEM

In thinking things through, it's a good idea to make a list of your top complaints about living with your spouse. Study these complaints. Are you sure a divorce is the answer?

I make a point of asking my clients to explain as much as they can about why they are unhappy. This gives me critical information I can learn no other way. If there are underlying issues affecting my client's assessment of the marital situation, I need to know it.

What if the real cause of unhappiness lies somewhere else entirely? Is your spouse unhappy with his or her work situation? Are you coping with a series of miscarriages? Dealing with an addiction?

Divorce isn't always the solution. Even if divorce is the right approach, an underlying issue could work against my clients' best interests. I care what the truth is. If the other side knows the truth—and he or she does—I'm going to be blindsided in court, and it may hurt my client's case.

No matter how painful or embarrassing the truth is, I need to know it. I've learned that very often a client is so deeply sunk into a miserable situation that the first story I get from him or her is not the one that will give me the perspective I need.

This is nothing new. Marriage counselors know a client's presenting problem may not be the real issue. It is a problem all right, but perhaps not the one that is really driving the discord. This happens because the client is unable to get enough perspective on the painful life situation to think clearly and identify the major contributing source of their personal pain. The counselor listens, thinking the presenting problem may be the driving problem, or it may be a side issue, but it is almost certainly just the tip of the iceberg. It is the job of the counselor to go deeper and find a way to pull the sheet off the core problem. Sometimes a divorce lawyer needs to use these skills as well.

Realizing that law school never taught me these skills, I decided I needed more education if I was going to be the best family law attorney and mediator I could possibly be. So I sought out the highest-rated mental health educational program in the country, the Menninger Institute,[1] and enrolled in a two-year program in marriage and family therapy.

My application was initially rejected. They told me they had never had an attorney apply before and couldn't see how knowledge of marriage therapy could be useful to a lawyer. I contacted previous graduates of the program, all of whom were mental health

---

[1] The Menninger Institute moved from Topeka, Kansas, to Houston, Texas, in 2003, and its professional training programs are now conducted through Baylor College of Medicine.

professionals, explained my reasoning, and asked if they would write a letter of recommendation that I could attach to my next application to the institute. It worked.

Off I went to study in the Menninger Program, and over the next two years I learned a great deal about how families operate as systems, with each member playing certain roles. I could see that getting stuck in these roles explained much of the illogical behavior of my clients during divorce. In the years since I earned my certificate from Menninger, my success rate at settling mediated cases and winning what my clients wanted in court has skyrocketed.

Law school taught me logic and persuasion, but I discovered this was not the first thing my clients needed from me. They needed understanding, compassion, and hope for a better life to give them perseverance. They also needed help in acquiring goal-setting skills. At Menninger I learned how to meet their needs and have never regretted the time, expense, or effort spent learning about family systems there. It changed the way I relate to clients.

Let's say you are fifteen years into your second marriage. You come to my office saying you want a divorce because there seems to be nothing but tension and arguing between you and your spouse. We talk about the kinds of fights you have, and it reveals that the most intolerable thing for you is that your spouse gives you little voice in financial matters. That is certainly a valid concern. You're angry. You've decided to get divorced. You ask me to draw up the paperwork and start the proceedings.

But I continue to ask questions, very specific ones about income, assets, and expenses. I draw a chart and help you calculate how much you would likely have to live on after a divorce. It doesn't look good. Post-divorce, each of you would likely be living in rented apartments and driving beat-up cars, and your dreams of retirement would go up in smoke. You are dismayed and tell me you feel trapped. But we continue to talk. Maybe it's becoming clear that for some years now, your entire combined income is needed to cover basic family expenses, because the two of you have been living on too grand a scale for your financial reality. Divorce would end the constant bickering simply by separating you, but the financial burdens and misery would increase. Wouldn't it make more sense for you to seek financial counseling together about how to greatly reduce debt and expenses? Perhaps you are not the only one who's been feeling that finances are out of your control. Sound financial advice about a road forward could empower both of you in making decisions together to stop the financial drain. Isn't it worth a try? After making those changes and relieving much of the tension, you can reevaluate the state of your marriage. Divorce will still be an option, but you will be in a better position to figure out how to make it work. I offer to refer you to a financial advisor.

This hypothetical example is based on real experience in my practice. It happens about one time in fifty, most often in mediation cases. A couple will ask me to mediate their divorce, but after we delve into financial details and paint a picture of life after divorce, they realize they can't afford it. They go back home, and sometimes, three or four years later, they come back for a mediated divorce, only this time with clearer, more realistic thinking.

This is not to say that you should stay married just because a divorce would mean that you have to decrease your standard of living. But you should consider ways to solve standard-of-living issues without going to the extreme of divorce. If the amount of family income is the issue, either of you could explore the possibility of earning more or spending less. If your spouse is the only breadwinner, you could explore possibilities for you to earn income also. And if you are convinced you need to divorce, there are ways to approach it that will not result in one or both individuals falling into poverty.

PROTECTING CONFIDENTIALITY

In this book I use stories to illustrate much of the content that I cover about divorce. Unless otherwise noted, each of these stories are actual cases I have encountered in my practice. The content of each story is true; however, I have altered nonessential information to protect the identity of my clients. I have the utmost respect for my clients, their struggles, and their right to privacy.

So, to protect their identity, I have changed unimportant information such as names, ages, sexes, locations, number of children, and sex and names of children. However, these changes do not alter the reality of the events depicted in their case. Every narrative is true, and hopefully we can all learn from the life experiences and trauma my clients faced when divorcing.

One couple I worked with decided to stay together until the wife could finish nursing school, which would allow her to earn enough money to support herself post-divorce and share the costs of joint custody of the children. While she was in nursing school, they continued couple's therapy, working on the emotional issues of divorce while preparing for their ultimate separation. By the time the wife graduated and landed a nursing job, they had already worked through scores of issues during therapy and were well prepared mentally and emotionally to make the decisions involved in a mediated divorce (we will learn about mediation in chapter 5). Their patience and preparation saved them thousands of dollars in attorney's fees.

When the decision to divorce is new and tempers are high, it is easy to tell the lawyers to keep fighting over certain issues, without regard for the mounting cost. This couple managed to put the brakes on their anger, dispense with the drama, and pursue a rational, measured process that put them, and their children, in a much better place post-divorce.

Not every couple is capable of such an approach. A lawyer and his wife who came to me to mediate their divorce are a case in point. They were set on divorcing, but the wife, who had never worked during their married life, did not want the divorce to diminish her luxurious lifestyle. There were no children, and the husband felt there was no reason she shouldn't reenter the workforce to help pay for the costly house and pool she did not want to leave.

But this was a hard pill for the wife to swallow. With her husband sitting right across the table, she loudly said, "Look at him! Do you think I married him for his looks? Hell, no. I married him because he's a lawyer! My mom married a lawyer, and she never had to work another day in her life! That's what I expected when I married him. Now you're telling me I'm going to have to work or lose my house and pool? This was not the plan. I don't like either of these options."

She was correct, in one sense: Divorce means choosing between imperfect options. When a couple divorces, no one gets what they signed up for. It is the death of their dream. It is common for each party to think, *Life is not being fair, so there should be some compensation somewhere, right?* Well, I'm sorry to be the bearer of bad news, but life is not fair, and nearly everyone thinks they are getting the short end of the stick during divorce.

BEWARE OF MAGICAL THINKING

Many people who come to me seem to think some or all of the following:

- Divorce is going to be the answer to all my problems.
- Divorce will cost me money and be an unpleasant process, but after it's final, I will be just fine and so will the kids.
- After the divorce, 1 will be able to continue at the same standard of living.

If this is you, watch out. You are confusing divorce with fairy dust. Divorce is not going to solve all your problems, and it is likely to create more, for a good long while. Immediately following the divorce, you will not be just fine; it takes a long time to emotionally process what just happened, and this is true for your kids as well. And unless you are extremely wealthy in your own right, you are going to have to get used to watching your pennies and taking your lifestyle down several notches.

Here's what Judith Wallerstein had to say in the book she co-authored with Sandra Blakeslee, *The Unexpected Legacy of Divorce: A 25-year Landmark Study.*

"Divorce begins with the escalating distress of the marriage breaking apart—a crisis that often peaks when divorce papers are finally filed and served. It creates several years of disequilibrium for everyone in the family. Many parents say that the low point doesn't occur until two years after the divorce … and if you are yourself a child of divorce, your own journey down this road will be complicated by your earlier life experiences."

In this case, finally convinced that she must move to a smaller house, she went around with a realtor looking at $500,000 houses. "They're all dumps," she complained. Ultimately, she cashed in a portion of the retirement funds she received in the divorce and bought herself a $750,000 house. She still refused to get a job and went husband-hunting instead.

Let's take another example. You come to me saying you need a divorce because you and your spouse have not been getting along for some time. You argue over many things, but the bottom line is that you feel your spouse doesn't respect you and or the contributions you make to the marriage. The love you once had for one another must be gone, you say, because how can there be love when one spouse doesn't respect the other?

I help you talk it through, and I bear in mind that I am only hearing one side of the story. The questions I pose are meant to help you arrive at a realistic and balanced assessment of the marriage.

Divorce is drastic, painful, and potentially costly. I want you to be aware that a good family counselor might be able to help you and your spouse resolve the issue and communicate better with one another. I offer to refer you to a marriage and family therapist. The bottom line is that if you blame your spouse for all the problems in your marriage, it is wise to question yourself carefully, or seek a counselor who can help you do so. Problems in any relationship are also learning opportunities. You may surprise yourself with what you learn that can help you improve your relationship with your spouse and others. Even if your marriage ends in divorce, you will be better prepared to weather this crisis and keep yourself from repeating poor choices or negative patterns in the future.

I am not a professional therapist and don't try to be. I am a counselor at law. It's my job to try to get my clients the best outcome possible under the law, whether its protecting them from an abusive spouse, protecting them from a false claim of abuse of their spouse, helping them plan an exit strategy from a bad marriage, or using all my experience and training to ask questions that help them see that getting a divorce is not going to solve the problem that brought them to my office.

MYTHS ABOUT DIVORCE

If my spouse and I battle out our divorce in court, the transcript of the proceedings and all the evidence will be kept private.

Wrong! In litigated divorces, everything that comes before a judge is a matter of court record, and nearly anyone can gain access to it. If privacy is a top concern, consider mediation.

During my divorce case, I will be able to speak directly to the judge.

Wrong! Only the lawyers speak to the judge.

It is always better for the kids if the parents stay together, rather than getting divorced.

Wrong! This is what everyone used to think, before mountains of evidence proved them wrong. Children are damaged most by conflict between parents that happens in front of them. If divorce can restore peace to the child's household, and if the divorced parents conduct themselves in a civil manner as they go forward in co-parenting, the children can thrive.

The Second Secret

"50 WAYS TO LEAVE YOUR LOVER"[2]

After considering the questions and issues presented in chapter 1 regarding seeking out the true roots of your unhappiness, and after coming to a clear decision that a divorce will help you live the life you're entitled to, the next step is to decide which method of divorce will help you gain your freedom with the least amount of conflict, trauma, and expense. This chapter will explain the advantages and disadvantages of the several different methods of divorce, so you can wisely choose the divorce process that best fits your needs and desires. There is more than one way to divorce, and that is what this chapter is about.

1. non-contested divorce
2. pro se divorce
3. mediated divorce
4. collaborative law divorce
5. litigated divorce

---

[2] Song by songwriter/singer Paul Simon.

No matter which method you use, here are the three major issue areas to be worked out:

- **Children**: This area covers custody (both physical and legal), child support, health insurance, and sometimes other topics that constitute a parenting plan: summer camps, music lessons, extracurricular activities, sports, cars, college expenses, etc.
- **Maintenance**: This is an amount of money to be paid by one spouse to the other for their normal living expenses. This is relevant when one spouse makes a majority of the marital income and the other has been out of the workforce for a long period, perhaps making a home for the main breadwinner or foregoing a career to care for their children, and therefore is entitled to maintenance from that high-earning spouse.
- **Property**: This area involves the division of property, assets, and debt.

The kind of divorce you choose depends very much on how your personal situation is mirrored in these three categories. But before I go into the different types of divorce, I would like to clarify something important. It concerns a term that is used throughout the country by lawyers and courts but is widely misunderstood by nearly everybody else. I'm talking about the term non-contested divorce.

Unfortunately, the name of this divorce is completely misleading. People infer from it that there is no disagreement between the parties. But the name non-contested really refers to the ultimate disposition of the case, and who makes the decisions governing property division, parenting, and finances.

If there is a trial, and a judge decides all these issues, then it's called a *contested divorce*. If the parties or their attorneys ultimately come to agreement instead of going to trial, regardless of how bitter the negotiations were, it is called a non-contested divorce.

Let's say Jack and Jill are divorcing. They both want the divorce, so that is not the issue, but they disagree on plenty of other things.

In ordinary conversational English, most people would say their divorce is contested—simply because they are arguing. Jack and Jill, like most divorcing couples, can find a lot of things to argue about. The fact that they argue, however, whether it's over the butter dish or the family beagle or the house on Maple Tree Lane is not the basis for calling their divorce contested.

So if arguing over the terms of settlement does not make the difference between contested and non-contested, what does? In fact, the difference is only clear toward the end of the divorce process, and it has to do with the role of the judge. Non-contested means that all matters under dispute were resolved through negotiation, and both parties are now in agreement about every aspect. In other words, the parties decided the terms of divorce themselves, as opposed to each making their case in court and leaving it up to the judge to decide. Let's look at two examples.

EXAMPLE #1

Reasonable Jack and Reasonable Jill differ over many things, but through common sense and horse-trading, in just a few weeks they are able to decide on terms of divorce they both can live with. Their lawyers bring the detailed settlement agreement to the judge, the judge reviews it, and if the judge decides the agreement is "not unconscionable," he or she signs off on it, and the couple are granted a divorce. As divorces go, this one has cost relatively little in attorney fees. There was no costly trial, and the timeline was also short: Jack and Jill were so reasonable that the attorneys didn't rack up a lot of billable hours.

EXAMPLE #2

Furious Jack and Furious Jill are completely unable to let common sense prevail over their burning desire to punish one another. Their lawyers fight bitterly for two full years, until the parties finally come to agreement the very morning of the trial. Yes, they have managed to avoid the eye-popping expense of a trial, but all those attorney fees from the prolonged battle—for phone calls, emails, subpoenas, depositions, court conferences with the judge, meetings, and so on—will set them back $250,000. Jack and Jill would have been far better off if they had adopted more reasonable attitudes and negotiated using a professional mediator.

Both of these divorces qualify as non-contested. About 95 percent of all divorces are ultimately classified as non-contested. The typical couple start out fighting over various things, gradually come to agreement, and the divorce is granted right before it otherwise would have gone to trial. The important lesson to take from this is that, to a large extent, Jack and Jill have the power to determine whether their divorce is going to cost relatively little or a fortune. The less reasonable they are, the more it's going to cost them.

Jack and Jill together have already spent a quarter of a million getting to this point, but if they can't reach an agreement on all points and the case goes to trial, they could be spending many additional thousands. And that doesn't even touch the divorcing millionaires. In these examples, we're just talking about Jill the teacher and Jack the plumber. How do they pay for it? They borrow money from family members; they go into debt; they cash in the kid's college fund; they sell the house. It's ridiculous. There are cheaper ways to get divorced, but people can be very angry and stubborn, despite their own lawyers' advice, or because they've hired greedy lawyers who encourage them to fight so the lawyers can bill more hours. Some divorce lawyers do that all the time.

When a client of mine wants to do something crazy, like cash in the children's college savings account to pay for a divorce trial, I refuse to do it. I'll tell him: "If you want to do that, you've got the wrong lawyer. Better get yourself a different one. It doesn't make sense to dissipate your assets on a prolonged legal fight, just out of spite. Don't pay me $300 an hour to fight for your beer mugs, just go out and buy more beer mugs! Use your assets to put your own child through college, not my child. It's not worth it to keep fighting and fighting. Just settle, cut your legal expenses off, and be done with it."

This is a very, very important thing to keep in mind as you are considering divorce. People do not start out with the intention of fighting crazily over trinkets, spending themselves into poverty, or acting unhinged. The stress of divorce can be terrible, and it drives a surprising number of people to behave against their own best interests.

I've seen this many times. I was involved in a mediated divorce case with a husband who fought with his wife over the weed whacker to the point of trying to strangle her—right in my office. He jumped across the conference table, grabbed her by the throat, and tried to strangle her. I stood up and tried to pull him off but could not break his grip. So I got my taser, hidden by the conference table, and pointed the red laser light right at his chest. Again, I asked him to release her or else I would shoot. He asked if it was a gun as the blood drained out of his wife's face.

"No, Jack, this hurts so much more than a gun," I said. "Sit down!"

His wife was going limp. I counted to three and pulled the trigger. Jack immediately let go, but only because his body had begun to convulse as though he had been struck by lightning. He flew over the conference room table and hit the floor.

It was about seven at night, and there was no one else in the office (you can be sure I'll never make that mistake again). I told his wife to go pick up their children from the babysitter and go to a hotel for the night. I told her *not* to go home. I explained that her husband would be on the floor for, oh, maybe fifteen minutes. When he stopped shaking so much I would put him in a chair, get him a glass of water, and talk to him about what just happened.

Then I would call him a taxi (before Uber, we had taxis) to take him home. His vehicle could stay in my possession all night. In the morning she had two choices: go directly to the courthouse and get an order of protection or pick him up and drive him back here to get his car out of the parking lot.

What was interesting is that the husband did not even need a weed whacker. He lived in an apartment and had no lawn to tend.

Another couple fought for hours over the aluminum foil in the pantry. Then there was the couple who spent $500 in lawyer time fighting over the garden hose, and another who argued endlessly over the raggedy throw rug at the bottom of the basement stairs.

I feel sure that if anyone had asked any of these reasonable, intelligent, educated individuals at some earlier point in their lives if they thought they would act so foolishly when negotiating one of the most important legal agreements of their lives, they would have denied it up and down.

You may be wondering how you—equally reasonable, intelligent, and educated—can avoid the same spiral into self-defeating, irrational behavior. Fortunately, there is something that can go a long way toward helping you handle the divorce process sanely: counseling. I strongly recommend finding a good counselor right now, as you are considering divorce. You will have someone in your corner, helping you weather the emotional storms. You will have the opportunity to talk out your anger with someone who sympathizes and also asks the right gentle questions to persuade you to stop sawing off the limb on which you are sitting. Seeing a counselor is not an admission of failure in any way; it is a recognition that divorce is one of the most stressful things in life, and it is only common sense to create a team of sorts to help you get through it in the best possible way. As mentioned elsewhere in this book, other members of your support team, besides your lawyer, should include a financial planner, a trusted friend or relative, and support individuals dedicated to each child.

Now, as to the kinds of divorce, I'll start with the fastest and cheapest and end with the most expensive and longest.

THE PRO SE DIVORCE

The fastest and cheapest way to divorce is pro se, which is Latin for "on behalf of themselves." No one hires a lawyer, so the expense is limited to a filing fee, which varies from state to state and from jurisdiction to jurisdiction within each state. (To find out the filing fee that will apply to your divorce, call the family court in the county in which you reside.) In a pro se divorce, the couple sits down somewhere like the kitchen table and decide how to divide their assets, their debts, and their parenting responsibilities, and agree they will each pay for their own living expenses in the future.

Who would be perfect candidates for a pro se divorce? Young adults and college students who are without much property. What do they have in the way of possessions? Orange crate furniture, secondhand futon, books, a laptop, an iPad, and lots of student loan debt. They haven't started a family yet. So let's say they got married during grad school and are getting divorced before graduation. They own very little. They haven't acquired debt together. They share the rent of the apartment where they live. They probably don't have jobs, but if one does, the money has probably been spent on food, rent, car, travel, and internet and TV access.

There just isn't much, if anything, in the way of jointly owned property to divide. Most of what they bought together were consumables such as food, gas, and utilities. If there are bikes, or a car, these were usually acquired before the marriage, or are gifts from family, or are borrowed. So how is their situation reflected in the three issue categories to be negotiated in divorce?

A. **Children**: Our example couple—let's call them Noreen and Nigel—don't have any children, so it's a nonissue.

B. **Maintenance**: This doesn't apply to Noreen and Nigel because they are equally poor and self-supporting, so one is not obliged to take care of the other. It's a nonissue.

C. **Property**: For Noreen and Nigel, there isn't any property to speak of. The assets have been spent, and the credit cards and debt remained separate: Nigel's credit card, Noreen's credit card, Nigel's student loan, and Noreen's student loan. There's just nothing to divide.

In almost every state, Nigel can go online and download a set of forms to fill out, which, when completed correctly, will be acceptable to the court. He can represent himself in the divorce. No lawyers. All he has to do is fill out these forms, writing down who gets what and waiving maintenance, go down to the courthouse, and file. He's given a court date, and on that date, he appears before a judge.

Before meeting with the judge, Nigel needs to make sure the sheriff served Noreen with the Petition for Dissolution of Marriage, which informs her about Nigel's request for divorce, provides the court date, and asks her to respond to all the allegations in Nigel's paperwork.

The court has a record of this service, because the sheriff is required to complete paperwork declaring the day and time the person was served. This is put in the court file. If Noreen fails to respond by the court date, and does not appear, it's not a problem. She was notified and given the opportunity, and the court assumes it is her choice not to respond, and to just accept the settlement that Nigel has set forth in the Marital Settlement Agreement.

After receiving confirmation that Noreen was served, the judge puts Nigel on the stand and asks him what I call the magic questions, which are essentially questions of identification: what's your name, Social Security number, were you married on this date, are you separated, have you divided all your stuff and your debts, is your marriage irretrievably broken, are you asking this court to dissolve this marriage? If Nigel answers yes to all those questions, he and Noreen are divorced. The judge just signs and hands him the divorce decree and he walks off, a single man again. Noreen didn't even have to be there, but by not showing up, she defaults to Nigel's plan for dividing assets, debts, etc. In most states, in a pro se divorce, the spouse is invited to respond to what the other spouse has filed but legally does not have to respond in any way. That's called a default, and it's perfectly fine. Attending the hearing is also optional. The court can send the divorce decree to Noreen in the mail if needed.

I've helped a lot of students get divorced. When they come to me and I hear the circumstances, I tell them they don't need a lawyer. I give them the website where they can download the form, and they're ever so grateful. However, it may be a difficult form to fill out. In my jurisdiction in Missouri, it's sixty pages long. The problem is that the form requires choosing among options at certain points, and those options may be described in dense legalese that sometimes requires expert interpretation, especially for students from other countries. One option is to contact the court in your jurisdiction and ask if they offer pro se clinics where legalese is explained and questions can be answered.

A WORD ABOUT WHOSE PROPERTY IS WHOSE

Having looked at the simplest of all divorce circumstances, let's get more complicated. Before we move on to the next method of divorce, however, we need some background. There are some all-important legal concepts of property to consider. Some of the knottiest problems in divorce concern how to divide up the stuff: What's hers? What's his? What's theirs? It can get confusing, based on the laws of the state in which the petition for divorce is filed. In fact, even figuring out which state's laws govern the divorce may be far from easy. The petition must be filed in the state of legal domicile (or permanent legal residence), which may not be the place where the couple are currently residing.

Maybe a couple has homes in several states. Or maybe they are a military couple, with permanent residence in two different states while they are living in yet another, or overseas. In such cases, there may be a choice of which state is the best one in which to file for divorce, and if you are in doubt about which set of laws is best for your purposes, it's best to consult a lawyer.

How your property is divided in a divorce depends first on whether the state in which you will file is a community property state or an equitable property state. At the time of this writing, there are only ten community property states: Alaska, Arizona, California, Idaho, Louisiana, Nevada, New Mexico, Texas, Washington, and Wisconsin.

Community property is a marital regime under which most property acquired by a couple during their marriage is presumed to be owned jointly by the married couple. However, there are exceptions to this general presumption, which we will discuss later in this chapter. In many community property states, statutes strictly mandate that community property must be divided equally between the spouses.

The court is prohibited from giving one party more than 50 percent of the property, even if that party is financially disadvantaged compared to the other spouse, or disabled, or was abused by the other spouse, or for some other reason the judge would prefer them to receive more. The judge simply does not have the luxury of helping one spouse more than the other.

All the other forty states, at this writing, are equitable property or non-community property states. Equitable property states allow property to be divided in an equitable manner based on the judge's discretion, whether or not that amounts to an equal division.

The court's labeling of property as marital or separate can have significant consequences. Marital property is typically divided 50/50 between the spouses upon divorce. Separate property, in many jurisdictions, is defined as

1. property owned before the marriage;
2. property acquired by one spouse during the marriage via inheritance; or
3. property acquired by one spouse during the marriage via gift.

If a spouse can prove to the court that certain property meets one of these three definitions, the court "sets aside" that property, assigning it to its true owner, and does not divide it between the spouses. Now, there are numerous exceptions to this rule that property acquired under one of the above three methods remains separate property. For instance, if a spouse receives an inheritance (separate property) but comingles it with marital property, that spouse may have lost the separate property exclusion by combining it with previously owned marital property. Now the court sees all as comingled marital property to be divided equally between her and her spouse. She did this unintentionally, but ignorance of the law is no excuse.

To cite an example: if Freddy receives an inheritance of $40,000 from his grandpa and keeps it intact, in a separate bank account just for that purpose and never adds marital money to it and the money never generates any interest income, it will be considered separate property when it comes time to divide assets. But if Freddy invests it into the retirement investment fund that he and his wife have been using for years, it is comingled and must be divided between them. Because there are so many court-made laws, so many variations from state to state, and so many nuances regarding separate property, readers for whom separate property could be an issue are strongly advised to discuss this with their attorneys.

To recap, every state is either a community property state or an equitable-property state. In a community property state, all property acquired during the marriage must be divided equally between the spouses by the judge. In an equitable-property state, the property a couple acquires during the marriage (i.e. marital property) can be divided *equitably* but not necessarily *equally* between the spouses. The judge can take certain factors into consideration and decide to award one party more than 50 percent of the marital property. The kinds of factors the court may take into consideration may include, among others:

- the ages of the parties;
- the level of education attained by each party;
- the marital misconduct of either party;
- whether one party stayed out of the workforce for a significant period in order to care for the parties' children; and
- the earning capacity of each party.

This list is not exhaustive. There are many other factors a judge could find significant enough to tip the balance.

The following hypothetical story illustrates how a divorce could feel very different for a couple, depending on whether they are getting divorced in a community property state or an equitable property state.

Tony and Tanya have been married twenty years and have two girls, one in high school and one in middle school. Tanya has been having an affair with a neighbor and finally breaks down and confesses to Tony. Tony wants to repair the marriage and suggests they go to a marriage counselor, but Tanya is madly in love with the neighbor and wants a divorce. For the past twenty years Tony has been working very hard, rising to top management, while Tanya stayed home with the girls. Tony pulls in about $500,000 a year. Tanya only works part time, teaching aerobics, with negligible income. Their lovely house is worth $750,000 and carries a large mortgage payment. They also have two luxury cars, savings accounts, and investments, and Tony has been accumulating a generous retirement account from the company.

VERSION 1: IN A COMMUNITY PROPERTY STATE

Tony hired me to represent him in the divorce. All the assets amassed by Tony and Tanya during their marriage are considered marital property under the laws of their state. Tony is shocked to hear that exactly half their marital assets will go to Tanya. After all, he is the one who often stayed at work until midnight and worked nearly every weekend, while Tanya slept in with the kids and participated in all sorts of fun activities with them as they were growing up.

As he is reeling from this upset, I go on to explain exactly what this means. Under the community property laws of the state, if he wants to remain in their house, he will have to pay Tanya half its value in cash. She is also entitled to half of his retirement fund and half of their savings and investments. In addition, he will have to pay Tanya monthly maintenance and child support for the girls, and he will only get to see his daughters 50 percent of the time. After hearing all this, Tony asks me, with tears in his eyes, how this could possibly be fair. Tanya is the one who strayed from the marriage, and he doesn't even want the divorce.

I sympathize but explain that although this may not feel fair, it is the law. If he decides to fight it, he will be spending money uselessly, because the judge is required by law to divide their marital assets exactly evenly.

VERSION 2: IN AN EQUITABLE PROPERTY STATE

Under the very different laws of this state, the judge does have some latitude to divide the property in a way that is not exactly equal. The judge could, if he or she sympathizes with Tony, grant him more of the equity in the house, more of the retirement account, and so on. The judge might rule that Tanya is not entitled to receive as much maintenance as she's asking, because she is able-bodied and relatively young and should get a job to help support herself and the girls.

This makes Tony feel a little better, but of course his anger, frustration, and sadness are still there. He says, "I still just don't get it. I'm a faithful husband and a great provider, and I love my family. Then Tanya cheats on me, and it's like a bomb detonated in the middle of my life. I've tried so hard, and with one stroke of a judge's pen, I lose my wife, my family, holidays with my kids, half of everything I own. On top of that I have to pay her money every month for maintenance and child support. I could lose my job tomorrow and no longer be able to afford to live in my house. And the judge thinks that's fair?"

"Yep," I say.

And in truth, it could have been a lot worse for Tony—or a lot better. As I discuss elsewhere in this book, you never know which judge will be assigned to your divorce case, how the judge you get will see things, what biases the judge may carry, or how the judge is feeling on a given day. Between the law itself, the unknown human element, and the liberal discretion given to most family court judges, there is a great deal that is simply out of your hands.

Divorce is hard.

Of course, it's not only very rich folks who are affected by the laws governing separate property. Every couple divorcing in an equitable property state can potentially be affected, even our poor graduate student couple, Noreen and Nigel. Let's delve a little deeper into the fact situations where one party declares property as separate property.

1. **Property acquired prior to the marriage.** Suppose that before she went to grad school, Noreen had a five-year career as a professional poker player. She took her earnings and invested them in artworks. If she simply continues to own them, and does not sell them, then at the time of divorce these would still be considered her separate property, and none of it would be awarded to Nigel. But if she sells one of those artworks during the marriage and mixes the proceeds into a joint bank account, it is joint property and will be divided equally between husband and wife. If she sells the artwork and keeps the proceeds entirely separate, in a bank account her husband cannot access, and the account accrues no interest, it remains hers.

2. **Inheritance.** Let's say grad student Noreen's grandfather dies while she is married to grad student Nigel. The money goes directly into a mutual fund account with solely her name on it. She does not touch the money, does not add to it at all. When she and Nigel decide to divorce, however, the interest earned on that money—for example, the quarterly interest—better not have been rolled over into the principal to help it grow. This is because courts can view the interest earned on separate property as marital income, so it must be withdrawn and used, or put into a joint marital bank account. Now, Noreen, like most people, did not know about this intricate part of the law at the time she inherited, so she never withdrew the interest earned and mingled it with the other marital money in the joint bank account. She also had no idea she and Nigel would end up getting divorced. It may seem unreasonable for a court to divide Noreen's inheritance just because she didn't do what she didn't know to do in advance of something she didn't know was going to happen. This is where things vary from court to court and judge to judge. Most likely it will be up to the individual judge in the case to decide if Noreen's inheritance is hers alone, or if it must be shared with Nigel. Sometimes judges just figure out the interest earned on the inheritance, move it over to the

marital property column, and let Noreen keep all the rest, as her grandfather intended. And sometimes they don't, especially if there has been a lot of comingling. Judges have a lot of discretion in how property is divided in divorce.

3. **Gift**. Now let's consider what would happen if Noreen's doting grandpa doesn't die but just wants to give her, and every other grandchild, a gift of $1,000 each. Many people try to dissipate their assets in their elder years, so that they can enjoy the pleasures of giving, and also because they want to diminish inheritance taxes for the eventual inheritors. In such cases, the gift, whether it is received before or during the marriage, remains separate property, unless the recipient moves it into the joint marital account, or uses it to buy marital property—say, in Noreen and Nigel's case, a down payment on a car, putting both their names on the car title. That use of the money makes the car marital property. Even if Noreen keeps the $1,000 in a separate personal bank account, the interest on the money, as previously described, is marital property.

So how do you know if the state in which you intend to divorce is a community property or equitable property state? The surest way, since these things are not fixed in stone and new laws are enacted all the time, is to research it yourself. Make sure you are using a trustworthy, up-to-date site. Much of this information can be found on the Internet on sites such as Legal Zoom. Or you can find a good domestic-relations lawyer and ask all your questions.

One of the toughest fights for lawyers is over what is separate property and what isn't. That fight can cost a lot of money. Very complicated cases often require forensic accounting, in which specially trained outside accountants are hired to put together a comprehensive picture of all assets and determine what has and has not been comingled. Unfortunately, forensic accounting is very, very expensive.

MONEY MATTERS

Financial advisors are not just for rich people.

Even if you feel poor or fear that a divorce will leave you impoverished, you would be wise to see an advisor. This might involve as few as two meetings: At the first meeting you will describe your situation to the advisor, who will then ask you to email or deliver specific financial documents so that he or she can bring the situation into focus. At the second meeting, the advisor will give you the analysis of the situation and point out the risks. By the time you leave, you should have a pretty good sense of the road ahead, a list of steps you can take in the short term and over the long term to rebuild your security and provide for your children, and an approximate timeline for achieving your list of objectives.

Money matters are stressful, especially in the wake of a divorce. Be aware you have a choice. You can abandon yourself to this harrowing situation, as though desperately treading water blindfolded, clueless about the depth of the water, the nearness of shore, or what might be swimming toward you. Or you can keep your head up and your eyes open and swim confidently to the next place of safety.

Sometimes the spouse who is not represented by an attorney will hire another attorney for a couple of hours to go over the settlement agreement and give a second opinion, to make sure it is fair and equitable. I recommend this. It's perfectly possible to hire an attorney for one task, as opposed to hiring an attorney to fight to the end. In many jurisdictions, this is known as a limited representation agreement. It is a good idea for the spouse to seek this in order to be sure of getting a fair shake, and understanding rights and consequences. At the very least, it buys peace of mind.

If the second opinion is positive and both spouses are comfortable with the agreement, they sign it, I sign it, I take it to the judge for approval, and it's all done. This is a pretty inexpensive way to get divorced—but only if the clients are reasonable.

LIFE HAPPENS

Many of the tips in this book are about what you can think about, find out, or undertake in the days and months ahead. It is wise to seek out the information and counseling you need going forward. But don't kid yourself; you are going to be blindsided, no matter what. The car's brakes fail. Your employer furloughs a good third of the employees, including you. Your oldest starts hanging with the wrong crowd. Your identity is stolen. The dog develops a malignant tumor. Your mother breaks a hip. Life happens.

Now, these things all may have happened even if there had never been a divorce—but everything looms larger and feels more threatening when you are on your own with no partner to help you shoulder each new challenge.

So, in view of the certainty that life is going to happen, what can you do to protect yourself? Line up your support network.

- Find an attorney, a therapist, a financial advisor.
- Put your closest friends on speed dial.
- Join a group of likeminded people, or a support group, so you do not go through this process *alone*.

MEDIATION

Mediation costs more than the almost-do-it-yourself divorce but still only a small fraction of what a courtroom battle entails, and it is designed to handle more complicated situations where there are disputes concerning many items concerning property, maintenance, or children. The ideal candidates for mediation are two spouses who need help in resolving matters in dispute but who are motivated to come to agreement in an equitable way in order to avoid all-out war in the courtroom. They want to settle their own divorce, but they can't come to agreement on things because they always end up fighting.

However, these two are rational enough to allow the mediator to shift their thoughts away from anger and resentment and focus them on the specifics involved in designing separate, sustainable futures for themselves while providing their children with the care and support they require. In other words, suitability for mediation covers a huge percentage of divorcing couples, no matter whether they are bus drivers, stockbrokers, or stay-at-home caregivers with spouses who are sole earners.

But keep in mind that mediation is not appropriate for everyone. There are three circumstances in which mediation is not appropriate:

1. **Domestic violence.** If there has been any domestic violence between the spouses, mediation is usually not advisable. The damaging power imbalance of their lives together inevitably casts a shadow over negotiations like an implied threat. The abused spouse may be under pressure by the abuser to capitulate to certain terms or might just be fearful that if the abuser's desires are not met in full, there will be consequences (see chapter 6). Put another way, if Party A is making decisions based on placating Party B instead of on what Party A really needs and wants, then Party A is acting out of fear rather than self-determination. The core concept of mediation is self-determination. If a party feels unable to freely determine what is best for his or her future, then mediation is the wrong method of divorce to pursue.

2. **Mental illness.** If a party suffers from a mental illness that prevents him or her from making wise decisions about the future, that person is not suited to a process of self-determination. Uncontrollable fear, paranoia, phobias, psychotic splits, voices

in the person's head controlling behavior, or the urge to self-harm are examples of mental states that interfere with a person's ability to make sound choices. Just to clarify, taking prescription medication to help you with depression and anxiety, which are commonly experienced during the divorce process, does not mean you are crazy and incapable of self-determination. If you are taking a medication to help you sleep at night, you are not mentally ill and incapable of making sound decisions about your future.

3. **Substance abuse.** For mediation to function as designed, both parties need to have clear minds capable of understanding the consequences of their decisions. Mind-altering drugs or intoxicating levels of alcohol interfere with the clear thinking required in considering life-changing choices. This is obviously unwise, so I try to screen for such conditions and suggest the couple use a process other than mediation for their divorce.

What if none of those circumstances apply in a given situation, and both spouses are fairly reasonable? Why do they even need a mediator? Why aren't they better served by the almost-do-it-yourself divorce?

There are a number of reasons we could mention. Perhaps their property division is too complicated for that method. Perhaps they need guidance from an experienced attorney mediator who can lay out options for their consideration that might never have occurred to them. Perhaps the spouses can agree on most things, but when it comes to child custody they are at loggerheads and don't know how to move forward.

Perhaps the spouses are very much in the public spotlight and want to avoid a courtroom battle in order to keep the details of their divorce private; what happens in a courtroom is always public record, while what happens in an attorney's office is completely confidential. One very common reason is that when spouses sit down at the kitchen table to make decisions about who gets what, they fight and nothing gets decided. By contrast, in an office setting, with a mediator walking them through the process, they behave better. The mediator also educates them about their rights, and puts legal options on the table for every conflict they have. A good example of this is the story about the husband who moved out of the marital residence into a loft with his new girlfriend. When his ten-year-old son came to visit, the child slept in a sleeping bag in the middle of the living room floor, allowing him to hear this father having sex with the girlfriend. The son eventually refused to spend the night with the dad. Dad accused mom of "parental alienation." Mom swore that she was not talking badly about the dad. After putting lots of options on the table to try to resolve this issue, it came out that Dad had a girlfriend staying at the loft, and they were particularly loud while having sex. Son didn't think he could tell Dad what to do and didn't want to tell Mom that Dad had a girlfriend while he was still legally married to Mom. Once both parents understood what was going on, they came up with a plan for Mom to pick up the son on Saturday nights at nine so he could spend the night at Mom's, and Dad could still spend the night with his girlfriend. Then Dad would pick up son from Mom's house on Sunday morning, and he could spend the whole day with Dad without being exposed to sexual encounters. This parental alienation could have been a $150,000 court battle when *neither* parent was trying to alienate the son. In that mediation I laid out lots of legal options for them to consider, and the husband and wife discussed each one and came to agreement on the best way to handle parental visits.

The cost of mediation varies around the country, but as a general rule it is going to consist of the mediator's hourly fee times the number of hours spent negotiating plus the hours spent drafting the legal paperwork for submission to the court. If the parties are rational and agreeable, I can pretty much get them to agree on all issues in about five hours, spread over three visits. Then it takes maybe ten to fifteen hours to prepare various legal documents: their filing documents, financial documents, a spreadsheet showing what they have agreed to, a final marital settlement agreement and parenting plan, and other documents for filing with the court. After that, it's ready for the clients to review.

Once they sign off on it, the agreement must be taken to court. The rules on that vary across the country and depend on the local court rules. In some jurisdictions, the spouses themselves can take the agreement to court and file, which saves them money. In some jurisdictions, the mediator is allowed to file the documents with the court. In some, the court requires one spouse to hire a second lawyer to take the document to court. Local court rules can affect other aspects as well. In some jurisdictions, the mediator is not allowed to draft the agreement that's just been mediated, which strikes me as ridiculous. The couple then has to hire a lawyer, not from the same law firm, to draft and file it.

Who are the best candidates for mediation? People who love their children more than they hate each other. They want to reduce the animosity, preserve any good will that is still there, and make it easier on the kids. They both still want to be involved in parenting their children. They go through divorce in a cooperative manner because they want to move forward in their new life in a cooperative manner. Court battles are very punitive; it's all about who's the good guy and who's the bad guy.

In mediation we don't care about who's the good guy and who's the bad guy. It's not about finding fault, it's about focusing on the future. In mediation we are not looking to find fault in the past or to punish for the past. We help couples design a future in which there is room for both mom and dad to be involved with their children, but lead their own lives. In the next chapter you will find a great deal more information about mediation.

RABBIT OR FOX? ADVICE FOR THE LESS ASSERTIVE

In choosing the right method of divorce for your situation, keep in mind that the complexity of the issues and the probable cost of the process are not the only considerations. Take your own personality and the character of your marital relationship into account too.

Is one of the issues in your marriage that you feel dominated by your spouse? Does your spouse constantly interrupt you, talk over you, undermine your statements? Does he or she register disapproval or disgust through facial expressions and gestures that make you feel small, inhibit your ability to think, and sap your will to fight? Does your spouse maintain a reasonable, calm façade but know exactly how to wear you down through endless talk?

In divorce negotiations, these are all truly dangerous to your interests. This is the time, of all times, when you need to claim what is rightfully yours. You need to steel yourself. Remember, the point of the negotiation is to secure your future wellbeing, not to make your domineering spouse stop talking. So if you are the sort of person who would rather cave than fight and you don't think you can manage a personality transformation overnight, consider the following:

- Avoid one-on-one discussions with your spouse at any time about any topic of your divorce.
- Do not allow your spouse to talk you into picking the do-it-yourself kind of divorce, where the two of you are supposed to work together, privately, to negotiate all points, and only one lawyer is hired for the purpose of drafting the agreement in legalese and filing it with the court. You will get screwed.

- Make sure that when you do sit down to negotiate with your spouse, there is a mediator in the room or your attorney is by your side. Either of these will stop intimidation by your spouse and make sure your voice is heard.
- Mediation, collaborative law divorce, or full-on litigation are better suited to serve your interests. You need either a referee or you need to hire an attorney to champion your cause.

THE COLLABORATIVE DIVORCE

In a collaborative divorce, each spouse is represented at the negotiating table by an attorney. The attorneys are usually seasoned mediators with at least four or five years' experience. There are usually strict rules regarding their qualifications, education, and experience in family law. Each spouse picks an attorney from a list provided by the Collaborative Law Association governing your region. Then the two teams of client and attorney meet and work cooperatively to come up with a mutually agreeable plan for their future.

Litigation lawyers—the ones who do all-out battle for you— look at every case as something one person is going to win and the other is going to lose. There is no in between. The mind-set of the mediator and the collaborative attorney is completely different than litigators; for them, both sides win. Their goal is to guide their clients in making sound decisions to create the best possible future for themselves in the wake of the wreckage. Many family lawyers do all these different kinds of divorce. They are simply adept at changing hats—and mind-sets—as the method requires.

So what kind of couple would be perfect for a collaborative law divorce? One that might be able to come to agreement on many issues but where one spouse feels intimidated by the other and feels more confident with an attorney sitting right there at every meetup to look out for his or her interests. A mediator can fill this need too, however. Like a mediator, the collaborative attorney will intervene to stop the negative interaction and will place a new option on the table for the spouses to consider. The conversation is always brought around to what will work for both parties.

In both the collaborative and mediation processes, the focus is on designing a future in which each party has enough money to live on and each party gets a fair share of the marital assets amassed during the marriage; there is room for both the mom and dad to be involved with their children but lead their own lives. Ideally, the clients also learn how to treat one another respectfully as they are guided through this process, peacefully and respectfully resolving one issue at a time. This is where the skill and experience of the lawyers makes a big difference. A good mediator or collaborative lawyer knows how to power-balance during sessions.

Here's how it is done: It's like a pendulum. One parent, let's say the mom, knows the following: (a) how to reach the babysitters; (b) when the parent-teacher meeting is being held; (c) who the new teacher is; (d) where the pediatrician's office is; (e) the list of kids' friends and their parents and their phone numbers; etc. She needs to write all this information down for the dad. He needs to know all this information and to meet those people. Dad, on the other hand, might know the following: (a) the monthly cost of the house; (b) their retirement plan; etc. He needs to pull all this information together for the mom. This helps parents realize their parenting interdependence and that neither can do their parenting job well without the assistance of the other. This sets the tone for the next ten to fifteen years they still have left to co-parent. *The greatest gift a divorcing couple can give their children is their obvious cooperation with one another and their commitment to keep any conflict between them away from the children.*

THE SCORCHED EARTH DIVORCE (AKA CONTESTED DIVORCE)

This is the divorce that goes to courtroom battle. It is the longest, most bitter, most stressful, and most costly. If you want to end your marriage in a way that is guaranteed to damage everyone involved, take years off your life, and transfer a big chunk of your wealth to a take-the-gloves-off divorce litigator, this is the method for you. It is also the method you will have to use if none of the other methods are suitable or your spouse is an unreasonable jerk.

One client (we'll call her Bellona, after the Roman goddess of war) spent about $35,000 in the first three months of her representation on an emergency hearing with the objective of getting exclusive custody of the house and the children, temporary child support, temporary maintenance support, and attorney's fees. That may sound like she was being unreasonable, but in this case, it was necessary. She and her husband, let's call him Mars, were incapable of anything but all-out war, and his was the only name on all the bank accounts. At that hearing I got her exclusive possession of the house and of her car, and her husband had to pay the house and car payments, all the insurance, and give her $2,500 a month in temporary maintenance, as well as $30,000 for attorney's fees.

From my point of view, as her litigator, it was a successful first skirmish, and it gained my client some temporary security as we prepared for the battles ahead. What happened after that, given the personalities involved, was one of the most contentious, furious, and unreasonably difficult divorces of my career. Over the next two years, each side burned through at least $150,000 in their pursuit of mutually assured destruction. Both Bellona and her belligerent husband, Mars, were willing to spend almost their entire savings and retirement funds to prove that the other spouse was a louse. Both took irrational, inflexible stands on many items of discussion, refusing to bend or compromise or negotiate. They fought over figurines, used paint cans, lawn equipment, used doormats, posters, food in the pantry, and old table lamps. Taking possession of something the other spouse wanted was their battle cry.

At one point, Bellona became so unstrung that she was frequently calling my office, and I never knew when I picked up the phone if she would be crying, wanting to give in to stop the fighting, or screaming about how she wanted Mars to suffer more. All the fighting and drama alienated the couple's several adult children, who didn't want any part of it. This case ended with Bellona and Mars harboring such hatred and bitterness that I doubt they will ever get past it.

I can envision them living out the rest of their lives in bitterness and resentment, using every family occasion to renew the warfare, unable to enjoy a child's jointly attended graduation or wedding, or to be present together for the birth of a grandchild. Both Bellona and Mars were already trying to pit their siblings against the other spouse's siblings—which could only lead to prolonged tensions and each child choosing to engage with only one side of the family.

What a sad waste of time, resources, and relationships! This is what litigation does. It pits family against family, brother against brother-in-law, and leaves the children, even adult children, with a greatly reduced extended family and damaged relations with their own parents. Litigation is the cruelest way to end a marriage.

The most important thing to understand in all this is that divorce is not one-size-fits-all. Your particular situation calls for an approach suited to the personalities and circumstances involved. You need to pick the right kind of divorce method and an attorney who is thoroughly prepared to proceed in a manner consistent with that method.

The Third Secret

THE REAL CASUALTIES OF DIVORCE ARE THE CHILDREN

Here is the truth you need to put front and center in your brain, now and forever:

Conflict between you and your spouse is poison for your child.

This is the indisputable finding of years of research across multiple disciplines. But note that this is not the same thing as saying that divorce is poison for the child, which was the prevailing view for a great many years.

THE RESEARCH THAT CHANGED EVERYTHING

We have known for a long time that divorce is difficult for children. The trauma of having one parent leave often gives rise to a gnawing fear: *If Mom can stop loving Dad, then she can probably stop loving me.* What a terrifying, corrosive thing for any child to think. It doesn't matter how many times you tell your children you could never stop loving them; on some level, they very likely still believe it could happen, and that is just one of many fears and other emotional responses they may have.

Divorce has been legal in the United States since the country's founding, but it wasn't until the 1970s that anyone took on the massive task of investigating just how it affects families with children. Judith Wallerstein and Joan Berlin Kelly, both clinical psychologists, launched their longitudinal research, the "California Children of Divorce Study," in 1971. They interviewed 131 children and their parents from sixty divorced families, when each divorce became final, and the family, as they had known it, ceased to exist. Then they re-interviewed them approximately every five years, and wrote books about their findings. The book summarizing their findings, *Surviving the Breakup: How Children and Parents Cope with Divorce*, was published in 1980. Its revelations about the negative impact on children caused a sensation.

The book became a best seller, but its finding that divorce was inherently damaging to children also drew volumes of criticism. Most critics tried to downplay the damaging effects of divorce, arguing that despite the sheer number of divorces affecting children, the world goes on. When one attacker said children were so used to divorce by now that they could lean on each other for support, Wallerstein famously retorted, "Children go through divorce in 'single file.'"

Having opened Pandora's box, Wallerstein continued her research, following up with each of the families in her original study. She and Sandra Blakeslee wrote about the effects ten years divorce in their book, *Second Chances: Men, Women, and Children a Decade after Divorce*. They explained that the effects of divorce on children are not transient but long lasting and profound, and they persist well into adulthood. Telling divorcing and divorced parents not to fight is not nearly enough, they argued. The overall quality of post-divorce family interactions involves far more than mom and dad fighting: Parents really need to fully co-parent and care more about the children's needs than their own.

Wallerstein and Blakeslee also found patterns of behavior according to the biological ages of the children in the wake of divorce:

- Two- to six-year-olds were terrified of abandonment.
- Seven- to eleven-year-olds were resentful when deprived of opportunities they would have had if their parents had stayed together.
- Eleven- and twelve-year-olds were more easily seduced into "street behavior" such as drugs, alcohol, and delinquent behavior, or they had to take on the role of a parent, becoming overburdened by the additional responsibility.

Wallerstein's continuing research culminated in the writing of her fourth book, *The Unexpected Legacy of Divorce*, which was the definitive report of her twenty-five-year longitudinal study. Again, the message was that divorce in itself is not what endangers children the most, it is *conflict* between their parents.

APPLYING THE FINDINGS TO YOUR OWN SITUATION

If you are in a miserable marriage with a lot of fighting and you know the children have witnessed this, does that mean you should quickly rush to divorce to protect the kids from the conflict?

Not necessarily. First you need to be very sure (see chapter 1) that in your situation, divorce is the right remedy for the right problem. Otherwise, everyone involved will endure a lot of stress, emotional upheaval, and financial strain, and after it's all over, the original problem will still be there, making you miserable. That's why you need to carefully think through the questions I've listed in chapter 1. You must be certain of the underlying causes of trouble in the marriage. If you are confused, the best thing you can do is seek out a counselor who can help you get to the bottom of it.

On the other hand, if there is any kind of abuse or violence in the marriage, you and the kids need to leave *fast*, and divorce is the logical step after safety is achieved. If there is no abuse or violence, but the situation is unhealthy for the parents or for the children, with slim prospects for improvement, then again, divorce may be the responsible course of action. For example, if the level of parental discord is very high, divorce might well be the right choice. Remember, it's not the divorce itself but the *parental conflict* that does the damage. If divorce is the best means of ending the conflict and enabling a healthier environment for the child, then divorce might be the best course of action.

No matter what you do, think through the potential effects on the children. Although you are keenly aware of your own suffering in the marital relationship and know what kind of toll it is taking on you, bear in mind that the consequences for your children are potentially worse and of longer duration, even if the kids are not showing it right now. Some of the effects on children include low self -esteem, plunging grades, depression, self-harm, inability to trust, and, later on, inability to commit to or to remain in a long-term relationship.

Don't underestimate the impact of divorce on your children. I once represented a client with several children born to her husband. One child was a bright student, star athlete, and well-rounded teen. When he discovered that his dad was having an affair with a younger woman, he went to his mom and said, "Mom, I'll never leave you." At that moment he was forced to choose sides and subsequently refused to see his father again. This happy, normal teenager with tons of friends and support systems at school ended up turning to drugs and later dealing them over the next few years. Eventually this child died of an overdose before graduating from high school. No one wants to believe this could happen to his or her child … but to these parents it did.

THE FIRST MISTAKE PARENTS MAKE

I've seen this over and over again. The first thing divorcing parents get wrong is thinking that they know exactly how their child is feeling at any given time, and exactly how the child is processing the divorce.

In fact, as we've seen, this may well start long before the parents initiate divorce proceedings, when the child is witnessing parental conflict. How much the child knows or understands about the discord is usually not the main thing on the parents' minds, but maybe it should be, because the child certainly picks up on the tension and is already attempting to make sense of it. What each parent says or does can affect the way the child processes what's going on.

Every step of the way, it is important to think through how your child could be affected. This includes the all-important moment of breaking the news that mom and dad are going to split up.

I've known parents who handled this exceptionally well: both meeting with all the children at the same time, explaining calmly, making sure the kids understand that the divorce is not their fault in any way and reassuring them that after the divorce, their dad will still be their dad who loves them, and their mom will still be their mom who loves them, and they will spend time with both parents.

I've also known parents who launched into decisions with potentially horrendous consequences for their kids, when they could so easily do things differently. Of course, this is often because, in the "fog of war" surrounding divorce when emotions reach extremes, stress is peaking, and the earth itself feels fragile beneath their feet, parents simply aren't thinking straight.

MONEY-SAVER DAD AND HOW NOT TO TELL THE KIDS

One couple came to me for a mediated divorce after twenty-five years of marriage and five kids. In several sessions we worked out the details of the divorce agreement. The mom would get custody of the children the majority of the time, as she wished, as well as monthly child support that would allow her to take care of them and keep them in their expensive private schools.

The dad had already bought a home for himself and had already cashed in part of his pension to pay off the mortgage on the marital residence where the wife and kids would stay. But the parents still hadn't broken the news to the kids that they were about to be divorced.

I told them that they needed to tell their children together, and that all five children needed to be told at the same time rather than individually. It's crucial for news of such magnitude to be announced by both parents, together, in person, because this lets the kids know that both parents are equally committed to the divorce and so both can respond to the kids' questions in a clear and noncontradictory way. And although it may seem logical to tell each child separately, adjusting for the age-level of understanding, telling all the children in the same meeting reduces the likelihood of damaging misinformation and misunderstandings.

The conversations with each child in a more age-appropriate fashion can follow in a day or two and continue as each child needs it. I told this couple that of course all the kids will continue to have questions or will need to hear the same information repeated over time—that's just how they need to process something so earthshaking. But telling them all together goes a long way toward establishing a shared understanding. Given the sensitivity of this task, I suggested to this couple that we role-play how they should do it.

To my surprise, the dad-we'll call him Money-Saver Dad-spoke right up, saying a role-play wasn't necessary because he'd already thought it through. His plan went like this: He would pick a day on a weekend coming up. That morning he would tell his older children (among them, three strapping boys in their teens) to load all his belongings into his truck, without explaining why. Then they would drive together to his new home, actually a cabin in the woods, where his kids would unload everything. Once the truck was emptied out, he'd tell them about the divorce and that he'd be living alone at this new house. Essentially, his boys, unknowingly, would help him leave them and their mom—with no advanced warning. These children would have felt like they had just colluded with their dad to help him abandon their mom and the rest of the family. Helping Dad leave the family behind would have been etched in the three teenagers' brains forever, making them feel like traitors by helping Dad steal away without Mom and the younger children. This was not Dad's intention. He was merely frugal and wanted, in his own words, "to use his young bucks' strength to save some money." He just never thought about this proposed action from his children's point of view.

There was no particular reason, he felt, for their mom to be present. He was particularly proud of his idea of getting the kids to do the loading and unloading to save on moving costs (said the man who was about to get a million-dollar bonus from his company for taking early retirement). I was speechless. His wife's jaw dropped.

My reaction was instant. The voice in my head was saying, *Well then, you might as well put all five kids in psychiatric institutions right now! No!* But thankfully, what came out of my mouth was, "You and your wife need to sit down and tell your kids together! And afterward you're going to use a moving company to move your stuff and on a day when the kids are not at home. It's devastating for kids to watch a parent moving out of the house!" I don't usually give specific advice like this in mediation, but I could not hold back my concern about the impact this plan would have on his children.

Fortunately, he soon came to his senses and agreed to tell the kids about the divorce alongside his wife. He also agreed to hire a moving company. The important thing to understand here is that the father was not intentionally trying to hurt his kids. He just wasn't thinking. But a lot of damage can result when parents fail to stop and think in advance about the best way to handle the situation for the children's sakes.

Children don't think like adults. Common sense tells you that they lack the decades of experience of adults and consequently can't get perspective on the problem. But there are other, bigger reasons.

For instance, do you perhaps think that your child is smart enough not to blame herself for the problems between you and your spouse? If your child is between the ages of approximately five and eleven years old, you need to understand that it is not a matter of IQ. This is the age group most associated with concrete thinking, a completely normal stage of cognitive development. As you might suppose, concrete thinking is very different from the abstract thinking associated with older teenagers and adults.

Abstract-thinkers are able to imagine alternative situations; they can more easily accept explanations that are outside their experience. But young children focus on what they can see, touch, and hear. Your eight-year-old boy may think, *But last week on my birthday they were smiling and laughing and had a good time when we went to the restaurant.* A child age eight cannot understand that one evening of pretend harmony—put on for his sake—does not outweigh years of destructive or negligent behavior, or whatever the issues might be.

He also might be thinking, *Well, if they got on so well at my birthday dinner, why can't they just decide to behave like that all the time?* The evidence he has observed with his own senses dominates his thinking to such a degree that he is unable to understand your abstract explanation, no matter how calmly and rationally you explain it.

Here's another hypothetical example. Let's say you and your spouse have a ten-year-old daughter, Dolly. On the fateful day, you ask Dolly to join you in the living room because you have something really important to share with her. You start by gently telling her that a big change is coming: "Daddy (or Mommy) is not going to live in the same house with me anymore." You tell her that Mommy and Daddy have been having trouble getting along, are working on their marriage, and need to take a break from each other for a while.

Hearing this, any child of ten is very likely catapulted into an extremely stressful state of confusion: What does "not going to live in the same house" mean? What does "working on the marriage" mean? What does "take a break from each other" mean? "Where will they be? Am I going to be alone? Will I still have a family?" It's confusing and deeply frightening. Now, maybe you both rush to explain, "Sweetheart, both Mommy and Daddy love you every bit as much as ever, and we will always love you and take good care of you." Then you both hug her and stroke her hair.

In our example, Dolly is very still. She lets you both hug her, but she asks nothing and says nothing. You might reasonably assume Dolly understood everything you just said and just needs some time to absorb it all. But did she really hear you? You may well have lost her after the first sentence or two. She doesn't understand any of it and her imagination has taken flight like a scared rabbit. She asks no questions because she can't process any of this.

Or, let's say Dolly picks up on the seriousness of your voice, or observes that you have been crying, and she starts to sob uncontrollably. Again, you might assume, wrongly, that she "gets it," that her tears mean she understands that her parents are separating because they are having problems of their own and that those problems have nothing to do with her. After all, she must have heard you two arguing, right? That means she already has a framework for understanding that everything adds up to an unsustainable marriage. Right?

Unfortunately, that's just not the case. Children up to approximately eleven years of age are not yet capable of thinking about the abstract cumulative effects of emotional conflict. They also cannot yet understand the abstract reasoning behind your chosen solution to the problem. You may be assuming that Dolly is thinking, *My parents are having* troubles *and they can't seem to stop, so being apart will help them be happier.* But Dolly just can't do that yet. Instead, she is thinking something you definitely don't want her to think: *They're breaking up because of me. It's my fault. If only I had cleaned my room when my mom told me to, they wouldn't be fighting.*

Children very often don't see themselves as separate from their parents' crisis. Instinctively, they look for their own role in the mess. This is why overhearing or witnessing parental fighting is so damaging. The parental argument is shocking and very immediate and the child forms an instant impression that is verified by her own senses, *Wow. Mom and Dad are really mad at each other! Mom doesn't want to pick me up from Brownies! Dad doesn't want to either! The only reason they're fighting is* me!

Not only are children unable to grasp the abstract reasons behind the split, they are unable to see that the problems driving it have nothing to do with them. Because children tend to think they caused the arguments, they often reason that the responsibility for resolving the conflict rests on them too. Of course, there is no way the kids can resolve it and when they see that they can't, kids younger than eleven or so do not conclude, the way an abstract-thinker might, that the problems are the kind that only adults can solve. Instead, they feel like their failure to resolve the problems they caused has put their family on the brink of collapse. Potentially, children feeling this guilty burden are vulnerable to a host of consequences, from falling behind in school to serious psychological problems.

Although the preceding examples are about the mistakes parents make when they break the news of a divorce or separation to the child, it is essential to understand that the problem is not confined to that announcement situation. *Parental conflict is damaging to the children whether it occurs before, during, or after a separation.*

If there is a war between the mom and dad, children become very confused about what they feel and what they "should" feel. In their logic system, it is not possible for them to support both sides, so they must choose a side. The child divides his loyalties between mom and dad, even though he may not be consciously aware of doing so. And then a lot happens at the unconscious level because how can a child pick one parent over the other without feeling guilty? Imagine a situation in which Mom has fallen in love with another man, so Mom and Dad are getting a divorce. Their six-year-old child, Christopher Robin, loves both his parents. But now Mommy has hurt Daddy a lot. So, Christopher Robin might well be thinking, in his concrete way, *I love Daddy, and Mommy made him so sad. I'm not supposed to love Mommy anymore.* This could be psychologically disastrous for Christopher Robin, not only in the near term but long into his adult life.

Even a small tiff between parents can trigger an avalanche of confusion and guilt. An argument between them that feels small to the parents nevertheless feels like war to children, who can't gauge where the anger will end. It doesn't matter what the argument is about. Children feel insecure when their parents fight. Worse yet, parents don't even have to fight out loud for the child to worry. Even an infant can sense the tension between his parents. I often have trouble convincing clients of this reality.

ESSENTIAL TIPS FOR HELPING YOUR CHILD BEFORE THE DIVORCE

1. Keep your child safe.
2. Seek the advice of experts and counselors, both for yourself and for your child.
3. Make as many decisions in advance as possible. For instance, know whether the marital residence will be kept and which spouse will live there.
4. Change as few things in the children's lives as possible. For example, try to keep them in the same school, the same neighborhood. Allow them to keep their pets, socialize with the same friends as before, and continue the same extracurricular activities. The fewer changes at one time, the better.
5. Don't argue with your spouse in front of the kids, ever. This includes phone calls.
6. Never badmouth your spouse to your kids, or to anyone else in front of your kids, or allow others to do so.
7. Let your child's teacher and school counselor know what is happening at home.
8. Announce the decision to divorce together with your spouse. All the children, no matter their ages, should be present. (For more suggestions on how to break the news, see my blogs during October 2016 on ConsideringDivorce.com.)
9. Be prepared to willingly answer any questions your child has, any time, even if you have answered them many times before.
10. Be aware that the divorce will have different effects on children of different ages.
11. Respect your child's feelings no matter what they are.
12. Be prepared for your children to react differently from one another. You can count on being surprised by their diverse reactions.
13. Make extra time to be with your child.

THE COUPLE WHO SPARRED AT HIGH ALTITUDE

Once I worked with a couple in mediation, both of whom had demanding executive jobs. Their child (we'll call him Bruiser) was not yet three years old and came to about knee level on his parents, who were each taller than six feet. Mom and Dad were working together very cordially, making good progress in mediation. They were already living apart, one in the marital residence and the other at a nearby apartment; Bruiser was moving back and forth between their two residences every few days and attending preschool during the day while his parents worked. I asked them how Bruiser was handling the separation. They both responded that he was having great difficulty during exchange periods, screaming and clinging to the ankles of the parent he had been living with for the previous few days.

I asked Dad if he thought Bruiser was being mistreated at Mom's house, and he admitted that this possibility had crossed his mind. But because Bruiser did the very same thing when Mom brought him back to Dad's house, he didn't think mistreatment was the issue. I thanked him for not using this as a custody ploy against Mom and then asked what he and Mom usually talked about during the exchange. These occasions were tense, he said, and they would complain to each other for a while, but he stressed that both he and his wife were civil and did not yell at each other. He doubted Bruiser could even hear what they were saying as he kicked and screamed on the floor at their feet. When I asked the mom, she said the same thing, and that although they argued, it was never nasty. All of this discussion, by the way, took place with both parents present. In mediation, both spouses together are my clients, and my goal is to help them come to agreement on the terms of the divorce. When one spouse answers my questions in front of the other, it helps keep them honest!

I told them that children can be very intuitive at Bruiser's age and can sense tension even if no one is fighting. As I spoke, I had an idea and asked if they would be willing to try an experiment. It truly was an experiment, because I'd never thought of this before, let alone had any clients try it.

"For the next two weeks," I told them, "do not complain at all during the exchanges. Instead, give each other three compliments while Bruiser is throwing his tantrum, six feet below."

They agreed to try, and I suggested we role play right there in the office. I started by asking the dad for three compliments he could give to the mom. He couldn't think of any. I happened to have a 4x6 inch index card on the conference table, so I grabbed it and said, "Come on, Dad. Give me three things you liked about her when you got married."

Again, he just shook his head and said nothing. So, I volunteered to think up compliments and write them down on an index card for each of them; then all they'd need to do would be to read the index card, several feet above Bruiser's tantrum, and see if giving each other compliments would make a difference his behavior. I said aloud, as I wrote on Dad's index card, "Gee, [mom's name]. I like your haircut."

Dad interrupted, "Well, what if she didn't have a new haircut?"

"Bruiser doesn't know that," I said. My next compliment for Dad's card was, "I like the way you've rearranged the furniture."

Dad broke in again. "What if I don't like the way she rearranged the furniture?"

"Bruiser doesn't know that," I repeated. I invited him to come up with a third compliment, but again, he gave me nothing. So I made up the third one and wrote it on the index card: "I like your dress; is it new?"

I went through the same process with her, who also could not think of even one compliment for him. Incredible. Both people were extremely good looking, very smart, and highly accomplished, and just a few years earlier, they'd been madly in love with each other.

After writing three random compliments for her to give him at custody exchanges, I had them practice reading the cards to each other. Both said they felt foolish and reminded me that they didn't really believe what they were saying. Nevertheless, they agreed to give this experiment a try for two weeks, whenever one was handing Bruiser over to the other. We made an appointment to meet back in my office, and I sent them on their way. I actually had no clue whether this would work, but I thought if even something as contrived as this could change the atmosphere around Bruiser from hostile to civil, the whole family would benefit.

Two weeks went by in a flash, and they reappeared in my office grinning from ear to ear.

Dad blurted out, "It worked like magic!" When he took Bruiser over to Mom's house, he said, "It didn't seem to matter that when I told Bruiser's Mom that I like her haircut, there was a bit of sarcasm in my voice. It still worked! By the time I read the third compliment off the index card, Bruiser stopped crying, let go of my ankle, and ran over to the couch to play video games!"

Bruiser's mother followed through with her compliments when returning Bruiser to Dad's house too, and the boy let go of her ankles, wandered into his room, and came out with a toy. The parents made a point of smiling at him, and each other, and the dad was able to leave without a problem.

Since then, as you might imagine, I've given other clients that same assignment. I have yet to be disappointed.

Parents whose relationship is unraveling are caught up in their own emotions and concerns about the future. It's not uncommon for stressed-out parents to subconsciously lighten the burden of worries they bear by simply assuming their child is processing the divorce just fine. They don't mean to do so; they don't set out to ignore their child's needs. They're just having a hard time focusing long enough on the child's reaction to pick up on any problems. But know this: It is a big mistake to assume the kids are handling everything beautifully with no lasting effects. That's why responsible, loving parents seek advice concerning their kids before, during, and after the divorce.

None of us are omniscient about what our kids are thinking or feeling. All of us are easily distracted by our own emotional burdens. This is one time in your life when you need to reach out and create a support team.

If there are kids, the kids must come first.

In the next chapter, we will look at the mysterious ways children can react to divorce and what parents can do to help them.

THE KIDS BILL OF RIGHTS

I have a right to love both my parents and want them in my life.

I have a right to live in a home where I feel safe.

I have a right to live in a home where adults find ways to disagree without conflict, and where adults respect each other.

When my parents decide to divorce, I have a right to be told by both at the same time, and with all my siblings present.

I have a right to ask any questions I want about the divorce, any time I need to, and to ask them again and again if I still don't understand.

It is not my job to be the messenger between my parents.

It is not my job to keep a secret for my parent.

If I am troubled or confused about the way my parents are acting, I have a right to receive counseling from someone who can help me.

I have a right to create boundaries around me so I do not have to witness conflict between my parents.

The Fourth Secret

YOUR CHILDREN MAY SUFFER COLLATERAL DAMAGE IN THE AFTERMATH OF DIVORCE

Divorcing parents often find themselves in a reactive mode, trying to parry one rotten blow after another. If the child is not overtly acting out—throwing tantrums, getting into trouble at school, crying uncontrollably, or refusing to speak—parents often assume everything is okay. That's what they want to believe, of course. But as most of us learned in school, the absence of a negative does not prove a positive. Assuming the kid is just fine is not responsible parenting, and it can have drastic consequences, as the following two stories illustrate.

THE CASE OF THE SECRET ON THE WINDOWSILL

In this case, the divorcing couple had been married about twenty years and had one child, a thirteen-year-old girl we'll call Minnie Jane. This was a collaborative law divorce, in which the couple and their lawyers were negotiating everything the couple needed to decide: division of property, financial support, and a parenting plan. The goal was to avoid any courtroom litigation. They were already physically separated; Dad stayed in the marital residence and Mom moved to an apartment in the same city. Negotiations had been going well up to this point, and the next topic to be addressed was the parenting plan.

That's when Mom showed up at a session in a state of fury and accused Dad of deliberately alienating their child from her. Since custody had yet to be worked out, Minnie Jane had been moving back and forth between her parents' places. The problem was that while the girl would go willingly to visit her mom, she refused to spend the night in her house and refused to say why. Mom accused dad of vilifying her. Dad denied this categorically and said he didn't know why Minnie didn't want to spend the night with her.

Because there was a mystery involved and the parents were not able to solve it, I suggested hiring a child psychologist to meet with the girl to see if she could learn what the issue was. This psychologist had a terrific way with kids that inspired their trust. The child opened up to her and the answer turned out to be something no one had expected.

Minnie Jane told the therapist she was afraid that if she spent the night at the mom's house, the police would come raid the house, and she and her mom would go to jail. It seemed the mom kept a small supply of pot on the windowsill in the basement where she'd go to smoke and blow the smoke out the window. She didn't think Minnie knew anything about it, but of course she did. In addition, she had just undergone DARE[3] training at school.

The police officer visiting her classroom taught her, "If you know anybody that does drugs, you have to tell the police. And if

---

[3] Drug Abuse Resistance Education (DARE), founded in Los Angeles in 1983, is an international program to prevent substance abuse and violence through education in the classroom and is typically used in sixth- and eighth-grade classrooms.

you are with them when they are doing drugs, you are going to get arrested too."

She didn't want to tell Dad that Mom was smoking marijuana while she was there because Dad would have to tell the police, and her mom would go to jail. And if Minnie Jane happened to be in the house when the police raided, she'd go to jail too. So she didn't tell anyone and bore the stress alone.

At the next client negotiation session, the therapist came too. "Here is what your daughter is afraid of," she said, and told them the whole story. Both parents were shocked and, of course, the mom felt awful.

After the revelation, we tried to do some creative problem solving. First of all, how could we help the daughter feel safe? Mom agreed to move the pot from the windowsill, keep it hidden when Minnie Jane came to visit, and not use it while she was there.

The child therapist met with Minnie Jane one more time. She told her, "You know, I met with your parents about this, and they're very sorry. Your mom is not going to smoke marijuana anymore. So you don't have to tell anybody, and your dad doesn't either, and you don't have to worry that the police are going to break in and take anyone to jail."

The next time Minnie Jane went to see her mom, the pot wasn't there and the overnight went fine.

In negotiation we came up with a parenting plan in which she stayed with her mom every other weekend, with one weekday overnight. Everything else worked out fine, the judge approved the agreement, and all was happy in the kingdom.

Not only did this relieve thirteen-year-old Minnie Jane of a lot of stress and restore a cooperative atmosphere to the negotiations, it kept the divorce process out of the courtroom, which was the couple's original intent. This saved a lot of tension and a lot of money, probably about $75,000 for each parent, because if we had not been able to learn and address the real reason behind Minnie Jane's refusal to stay with her mom, she would have fought the father for sole custody, and that would have been long and expensive.

THE CASE OF THE DAD IN THE LOFT

This case presented similarly to the case above. A couple with a young daughter was negotiating their way through a collaborative law divorce, with a lawyer representing each of them present at each meeting. Dad had already moved out of the marital residence into a loft in the city. The daughter—we'll call her Thumbelina—wanted to see her dad, but after a couple of visits she flat-out refused to spend another night at his place. As with the previous example, she was clearly uncomfortable but would not tell anyone why.

Again, we hired a child therapist to see if there was anything Thumbelina could tell the therapist that she was afraid to tell the parents. Sure enough, she was willing to tell a helping adult who was not her parent.

Dad had a girlfriend—a fact unknown to Mom—and she'd moved in with him. When the daughter visited, the girlfriend was there. When Thumbelina spent the night, she slept in a sleeping bag in the middle of the living room floor.

The loft had two floors, with a very open floor plan; the single bedroom upstairs had no door. You can guess where this is going: Thumbelina reported that Dad and his girlfriend would have loud sex in the bedroom upstairs. Very likely the sound would reverberate off the steel walls of the loft, so it probably sounded worse than it actually was, but this is what Thumbelina was hearing every time she slept over.

The daughter didn't want to tell him not to have sex. Thumbelina was only nine years old, after all, and she thought he'd get mad. She didn't want to tell her mom about it because it would hurt her feelings to learn that Dad was having sex with another woman while still legally married to her. Unsure of what to do, Thumbelina would visit Dad and his girlfriend in the loft and then would call Mom in the middle of the night to come pick her up. Dad failed to see the connection and leaped to the conclusion that it was all Mom's doing.

The therapist met with Thumbelina and then attended the next collaborative meeting of lawyers and parents. She said, "Here's what's going on: loud sex in the loft. She doesn't want to tell Mom because Mom will cry and be sad, and she doesn't feel she can tell Dad to stop having sex."

When the parents could catch their breath, I quickly offered a suggestion from my mediation bag of tricks—the kind of thing any good mediator would do to move the parents off the emotional hot button and focus on how to move forward.

"In order to solve this problem," I began, "I suggest we list all the different possible options and consider them one at a time."

1. Dad sends his girlfriend elsewhere when daughter comes over. Dad refused to do that.

2. Dad doesn't have sex with girlfriend on the nights daughter stays over. Dad, probably just to jab Mom, said that would be "impossible."

3. Dad and girlfriend could continue to have sex when the daughter comes over, but be quiet about it. Dad said that was impossible too, because the sex was "too intense." (That was another jab at Mom.)

4. Dad and daughter have their visit, but he returns her to mom's house at nine p.m. Dad didn't want to do this.

5. Dad and daughter have their visit, but Mom picks the daughter up at nine p.m. to take her home. Dad said this was the only viable option. He also wanted the option of spending more time with his daughter for a portion of the following day. Mom agreed to all this.

At that point, on the cusp of agreement, Dad's lawyer pulled him out of the room (by the collar of his shirt, literally) on a pretext, but it was clearly for a strategizing session. This is against the rules of collaborative law where everything is supposed to be out in the open, but I was sure I knew what it was about. Dad's lawyer was telling him that if he gave up overnights with his daughter, he would have to give up his discount on child support—so his monthly child support payments would be higher. So, when Dad and his attorney came back in, Dad said he'd changed his mind. He didn't want Mom to pick their daughter up, and he now wanted 33 percent of the overnights per year. I asked him how many nights that would be, and he had no idea what he was really asking for. This was a complete reversal of what he earlier had said he wanted.

When they first went out of the room, I turned to my client and explained what they were no doubt plotting out in the hallway in order for Dad to keep his child support payments lower. We figured out what the overnight child support discount would mean in dollars and it was a $59 a month loss for Dad if he did not keep Thumbelina overnight on Saturdays.

When Dad and his attorney returned, I said, "Well, if this is about keeping your overnights discount, we're willing to give you that whole discount every month even if you don't have your daughter overnight. We don't want this to be about money. Now, realizing you are not going to get docked money every month, do you want Mom to pick the child up at nine p.m.?"

And he said yes. I turned to my client and asked, "Would you be willing to let him keep his $59 monthly discount, even though you would actually be picking up Thumbelina at nine o'clock so that she won't have to listen to him having sex with someone else?"

She said, "Absolutely."

Problem solved. So we drafted an agreement covering division of property, financial support, and a parenting plan, submitted it to the judge, who approved it, and that couple got divorced in probably three or four months. Thanks to the help of the child therapist, we were able to get to the bottom of a mystery that threatened to pitch the case into a costly courtroom battle over custody, all because one parent was oblivious to the child's perspective and the other parent couldn't figure out what was happening. Fortunately, with a bit of guidance, the parents proved willing to negotiate rationally about how to resolve the issue, and find a solution that would work for them and their daughter without draining their bank accounts or ratcheting up to a level of bitter recrimination that would unquestionably damage all three of them, particularly Thumbelina.

IT'S UP TO YOU AND NOBODY ELSE

When I'm involved in a dissolution case that involves children, I give clients a quick overview of the results of the Wallerstein study. My client will nod in understanding because it just makes sense. But I always go deeper than this.

To make it personal, I ask them questions about their children and their hopes for their children's futures. I call it my parenting fireside chat. I actually move my clients to overstuffed comfortable chairs in front of a pleasant fireplace in my office. I sit in front of them and initiate the conversation. Instead of asking about their custody plan—because those are fighting words—I invite them into a much broader discussion about their hopes and dreams for their children. Often, I can see their shoulders soften, and they will smile. I ask them if they prefer private or public school. I ask them if they plan to pay 100 percent of college, a portion of it, or none. They talk with excitement about their child's sports activities, grades, and whether the plan is to buy the kid a car at age sixteen or save the money to pay for a wedding.

After they have immersed themselves in the fantasy of their children's future, I ask them, "Do you realize that if you continue to have an antagonistic relationship with your spouse, your child might pick your spouse as the 'good guy,' which automatically makes you the 'bad guy'?"

Bad guys are never invited to take the prom picture, watch sporting events, or attend a birthday party or graduation. This could be your future if your two-year-old decides subconsciously to align with your spouse instead of you. You probably wouldn't let your two-year-old decide what to wear in the morning, but that two-year-old is going to decide who is the bad guy in the divorce. You can't coerce this child; you can't buy this child; you can't persuade this child. The only thing you can do is make sure you are not pegged the "bad guy." This requires you to have a civil, respectful relationship with your spouse during and after the divorce. That's it. That's your only guarantee to remain an active part of your child's life. If you speak negatively about your spouse in front of your two-year-old, parenting for you could be over.

If I am looking at a blank face by this time I've gone over all that, I figure I got through to them. If I don't think they believe me, I give them a brochure designed by UptoParents.org,[4] a terrific online resource. On the cover is a picture of a toddler with a heartbreakingly sad face. The message inscribed above this angel of a child is

Parents:
If you are in conflict, your children are in danger.
And only you, their parents, can protect them from that danger.

In addition to advice and warnings, this website is packed with short videos of children talking about their experiences, stories of what divorce feels like from a child's point of view, and interviews with professionals (lawyers, mental health professionals, judges) that offer terrific insight about what our children need from us during the dismantling of their family. One of the maxims on the UpToParents website is: "Don't use your children as messengers."

I know this full well, and since I considered myself an expert on divorce, I wasn't prepared one day during my own divorce, after a fifteen-year marriage, to be upbraided by my own eleven-year-old daughter and taught a valuable lesson.

---

[4] UpToParents.org is a free website giving separated, divorced, and never-married parents the chance to build better futures through a single powerful strategy: focusing on their children's needs. The website was initially built by an Indiana husband and wife team, Charlie and Barb Asher, using their combined backgrounds in law, mediation, and social work.

One morning as I was getting her off to school, I tucked into her backpack a signed permission slip for her to go on a school field trip to the zoo. Knowing her father was going to pick her up from school that day, I reminded her to have him sign it also.

To my surprise, she planted herself in front of me, standing tall and with her arms down against her sides, and recited in a voice like an old-fashioned telephone operator: "I'm sorry. I am not your messenger. If you have a message for my father, please call him at [his phone number]."

I could not believe my eyes or my ears. I started to explain that it was "just a school permission slip" when she interrupted me and started the mantra over again. This time, I realized that this was probably something she'd been taught at Kids in the Middle, a nonprofit organization in St. Louis that provides individual and group counseling for children of divorce.

I picked up on her cue and said, "You are exactly right! You are not my messenger. I'm sorry I asked you to carry a message for me. I'll take care of it myself. Thank you for reminding me of my own responsibility, and please remind me if I forget this in the future. Great job!"

She instantly morphed back into my eleven-year-old daughter and started chatting about something else. After dropping her off at school, I went to my office and faxed the permission slip to her father's office with a short note, asking him to sign it and put it in our daughter's backpack for her teacher to retrieve the next day.

Afterward, I felt embarrassed that I, who certainly knew better, had tried to use my child as a messenger. But I was also grateful that someone had empowered her with those words. Wouldn't it be great if every child of divorce were empowered to recite a similar mantra to remind his parents not to put him in the middle?

Kids, so helpless in these adult wars, should be empowered to speak up for themselves. We adults get too caught up in ourselves and we make mistakes. I am no exception. As you'll see, this was not the only time my daughter felt the need to set me straight with one of her mantras.

There are many other ways of placing your child in the middle without asking them to deliver a message. It usually comes about when we get caught up in our own concerns and wind up thoughtlessly saying or doing something that unintentionally hurts our children. A case I mediated comes to mind.

THE DAD WHO OUTSOURCED HIS SECRET

This case involved a couple—I'll call them Jack and Jill—with a fourteen-year-old daughter. The family had lived in Chicago for years, but a job promotion moved Jack to Minneapolis. He agreed to the promotion as long as the Minneapolis assignment would not exceed one year. Jill and their daughter remained in Chicago, and Jack got a temporary apartment in Minneapolis. He flew back one or two weekends a month, and all seemed well. The promotion meant a nice pay raise, which would allow the parents to pay for the daughter's college when the time came. Both Jack and Jill said the separation was hard on their marriage, but they were willing to tough it out for the benefit of affording college for their daughter. Then the parents drifted apart, Jack's trips back to Chicago became fewer and fewer, and eventually, Jack wanted a divorce.

Their mediation sessions went smoothly, with Jack being especially sensitive and generous to the needs of Jill and their daughter. They came to agreement regarding the division of marital property, and came up with an "out-of-town" parenting plan and an arrangement on spousal support. The last issue on the table was child support.

When the parties came to what I thought would be their final mediation session, the past spirit of cooperation was gone, and I mean gone. Facing a wall of tension, I put the child support issue on hold and opened with a more general question about whether anything had changed between them since their last meeting.

Jill was only too happy to begin. "Well, since that last time we were here, I found out, through our daughter, that Jack has a girlfriend in Minneapolis. He bought a house there in her name so I wouldn't find out, and fathered an infant with ... this girlfriend! When our daughter flew up to be with him over the summer, she was introduced to this baby as her new little sister but told not to breathe a word to me because it would just hurt my feelings. I can't believe he put her in the middle like this, making her keep a secret from me."

Jack lowered his gaze to the floor as Jill continued: "She tried to keep the secret, but one night I went into her room to kiss her goodnight and she was sobbing. That's when she broke down and told me, apologizing profusely. How could her father be so stupid as to think I would never find out? I feel like this whole mediation has been based on a lie!"

Needless to say, that was not their last mediation session.

I suggested they cancel their session that day and take some time to integrate this new information, and they did. We met two more times and were able to conclude the mediation successfully. As I drafted their court agreement, I could not help but wonder what this experience must have felt like to their twelve-year-old daughter whose voice was not represented at the mediation table. If she could have been there to speak for herself and express her needs to her parents surrounding their divorce, I wonder what she might have said. My heart was heavy for all the unfortunate children who get tossed about by our legal system with the equivalent of duct tape over their mouths. Why? Is it because we don't want to hear how painful this is for them?

Parents' thoughtless behavior can injure their kids' long term. Jack's instructions to his daughter to *not* tell her mom about the new baby sibling in Minneapolis might have been intended to spare Jill's feelings, or it might have been intended to make things more convenient for himself. Either way, Jack made a huge mistake by making his daughter carry the heavy burden of a family secret. The fact of the second family would not have been easy on the girl no matter what, but when Jack put his daughter in the middle and swore her to secrecy, it became unbearably difficult for her.

LISTEN TO YOURSELF WITH YOUR CHILD'S EARS

Remember: Parental conflict is the demon, and you don't have to be arguing face-to-face with your spouse for it to count as conflict in your child's perception. Anytime you say anything disparaging about your spouse counts as conflict, because it feels like conflict to your child.

Children view themselves as being made up of part mom and part dad. Anytime anyone disparages a parent, they feel like the rude comment is being directed at them. In fact, what's going on with children might best be described as a ten-car pileup on the highway. A child has all sorts of conflicting feelings colliding at once: She feels personally rejected. She's worried that one or the other or both parents will abandon her. She's fearful that the hostility she's witnessing is going to escalate to something even worse. She feels personally responsible for the parental conflict in the first place and guilty for something she hasn't even done. She feels that she is the only one who can solve this problem, although she cannot. How on earth can she process all that?

One of the worst, most thoughtless things you can do to your child is also one of the most common: talking badly about your spouse in earshot of your child. As my daughter was preteen age at the time her father and I divorced, one of the only times I could corral her to find out what was going on in her life was during our forty-five-minute drive to her school. After a while, she would start talking on her own, just to break the silence.

One time, I was on my cell phone with my brother when I picked her up in the usual carpool line. Not bothering to notice what I was saying or where I was saying it, I started complaining about her father. And again, as practiced during her year at Kids in the Middle, she went into a mantra in her rehearsed telephone operator voice and said, "I'm sorry, but you're talking badly about my father and I can hear it. Please don't talk badly about my father when I am around."

I immediately hung up, apologized for breaking the rules, and changed the conversation to her school day.

Once again, I thought I was a seasoned divorce professional who knew how to protect my daughter as much as possible from the ravages of divorce, yet here I was, breaking all the rules. If I couldn't remember how to act, despite my law degree, my marriage and family counseling training, and all my experience, how could other parents? It is difficult to diligently follow all the rules, especially when you are under a lot of stress as a divorced parent. I turned out to be no different from anybody else and needed to be taught a lesson about how to conduct myself in a way that always put my child's needs first.

But this isn't just about how I needed to be set straight. The larger lesson I learned is one of the most important things I can share with you: Giving your children permission to stop you if they feel uncomfortable about what you are saying or doing is one of the best ways to keep you on the straight and narrow. As advised by Up to Parents, Kids in the Middle, and other organizations and educational programs on divorce, children deserve to set boundaries around themselves to protect them from hearing things that are too scary to hear and seeing things that are too scary to see. Parents need to encourage and respect those boundaries. It's one thing we can do to help them cope with the pain of divorce in their own time and in their own way. In addition, encouraging your children to intervene when their boundaries are violated has the effect of empowering them right at a time when they are feeling completely powerless. What a great way to help your children heal, teach them an important lesson about how to handle relationships in a mature and loving way, and strengthen your own relationship with them.

I encourage all my clients with kids to look well into the future and ask themselves questions about how they want their children to feel as they grow up in a divorced family. I give them a list of questions, some of which I've listed below. You might want to reflect upon them and even add them to your list of promises to your children so that your actions now can be consonant with the long-term results you want for your children.

- Five years from now, what do you want your relationship with your child to be like?
- Five years from now, what do you want your relationship with your ex-spouse to be like?
- Five years from now, what do you want your child's relationship with your ex-spouse to be like?
- When your child becomes an adult, how do you want him or her to think about long-term or marital relationships?
- When your child grows up and has relationships, how do you want him or her to handle conflict?
- What can you do now to help create these best future outcomes?

Again, I cannot take credit for these questions. I have selected them with permission from the multitude of thought-provoking questions posed by Charlie and Barb Asher on their amazing free website www.UptoParents.org. The work, research, and free information provided by the Ashers in an attempt to save children from the trauma of divorce is an amazing resource. Anyone working with clients facing divorce owes the Ashers a huge debt of gratitude for their contributions to the field of study of the impact of divorce on children.

A MOVIE WE CAN LEARN FROM

As an attorney, I spend my waking life making cases for one thing or another. So it's a delightful surprise when a movie comes along that makes my case for me.

Whenever I meet with clients in mediation, I try my best to get them to focus on the future. What kind of future do they want for themselves and for their children? Do they understand that what they decide right now, and the attitude they bring to this arrangement in the years to come, shapes the future for their children as well as themselves? That's the task before us: making decisions together that will create the healthiest, most financially sound, and most harmonious future for the divorced parents and their children.

Not rehashing who did what to whom. Not trying to make the other spouse as miserable as possible. Not laying the groundwork for a lifetime of battles with the kids in the middle or even used as pawns. If you allow vengeance and bitterness to govern your decisions and your attitude, you are poisoning the future for all concerned. Don't we owe more than that to our kids and ourselves?

It takes all my skill and experience to get these ideas across. So imagine my delight to discover a recent film that eloquently makes my case.

The title is *ACOD,* an acronym for *Adult Children of Divorce.* It may sound like a documentary about a new national self-help organization, but no, it is a fictional movie. The story centers on a young man whose parents' acrimonious divorce many years earlier laid the groundwork for an endless string of battles and fireworks, depicted with sardonic dark humor, leading up to the story's crisis and aftermath. Before I hit the highlights, however, I'd like to bring up a useful parallel.

Remember *A Christmas Carol* by Charles Dickens with its three views of Christmas Past, present, and future, meant to instruct the old miser Scrooge, who thought of no one but himself? Christmas past was tender and nostalgic, showing Scrooge the best moments of his own childhood. Christmas present was the unvarnished reality of the moment, in which Scrooge is forced to look in on the real-time consequences of his own miserliness and what other people think of him. Then, there is Christmas future, playing out all the dire and woeful things that will happen to innocent people, and the awful way he will be remembered, if Scrooge fails to mend his ways. Miserly old Scrooge, horrified into the intended epiphany, repairs his ways and redeems himself.

Watching *ACOD,* written and directed by Stuart Zicherman, himself a child of bitter divorce, is like a visitation from the Ghost of Divorce Future. Telling the story with the help of a vastly gifted comedic cast-not only Adam Scott and Amy Poehler of *Parks and Recreation*, but Jane Lynch from *Glee* and Catherine O'Hara from the movies *Best in Show* and *Home Alone* among others, *ACOD* delivers its cautionary message with dead-on caricatures and darkly funny interactions.

However, just to make sure audiences are aware that there is a serious intent behind all the comedy, the movie opens with a stark message. No music, just large white lettering on a black background:

1 IN 2 MARRIAGES ENDS IN DIVORCE.

THIS ONE ... WAS PARTICULARLY UGLY/ CRUDE/VICIOUS [SEQUENCE OF OTHER ADJECTIVES]

So, let me tell you a few of the ways I feel the movie, like the Ghost of Divorce Future, makes my case about how poor parental behavior and decision making can affect children:

1. Parents who put their own need to fight above the needs of their own child.

Scene: The son, Carter, as a boy, at his backyard birthday party videotaped by an adult guest, as the cake with flaming candles is passed down the picnic table to him. The happy moment is drowned out by the parents' obscenity-laden screaming from the lawn just below. A voiceover says, "On the occasion of his ninth birthday, over a store-bought cake, a simple wish was requested by the birthday boy: *Stop the madness.* It did not come true."

2. Parents who directly and indirectly emotionally manipulate the child.

   ("It's up to you, son. Who do you want to live with?") Who pressure the child into awkward, unnatural stepfamily relationships ("This is Chloe. She's going to be your new sister from now on.")

   Who indulge in groundless character assassination ("I hate to be the one to break it to you, sweetie, but your father is a homosexual.") [Obviously that scene is from a past time of less acceptance of homosexuality.]

   Who force the child to stand witness to the parent finding "true love" over … and … over … and over again in serial marriages.

3. Parents who continue to feed the flames of their mutual hatred, decades after the divorce.

   Scene: A high-end restaurant. Carter, now an adult of about thirty, has asked his mother and his father to meet him there for dinner, although neither parent knows the other is coming. Carter's much-younger brother has decided on a whim to get married and wants the divorced parents, who haven't spoken in twenty years, to attend. Each parent has separately refused to be in the same room with the other, but Carter, ever in his role of peacemaker, has contrived to have both parents come to a public place to try to negotiate their attendance at the event. After their initial horror at seeing one another and melodramatic threats to bolt, the parents sit down and stare at each other with simmering rage. Each accuses their son of destroying the evening.

Carter speaks. "Really? Look around you. The walls are still standing. You're both in the same room. And somehow the universe hasn't folded in on itself. Holy shit. Now I've brought you both here tonight because you have turned a nine-year marriage into a hundred-year war. And I am officially over it. We're playing by new rules now, okay? Trey is getting married. There is going to be a wedding. And all you have to do is show up, be civil, and for one night, shut the eff up."

One line from Carter's speech is my favorite because it sums up so much in just a few words: *You've turned a nine-year marriage into a hundred-year war.*

4. There are also scenes of "therapy," illustrating Carter's denial that he has any residual issues from his parents' hundred-year war. Carter: "My life and my parents' lives are completely separate. They have nothing at all to do with one another. No, my parents do not affect me at all." Anger, denial, a reluctance to commit to marriage, a self-imposed role of peacemaker and problem-solver for everyone around him: These are a few of the issues Carter carries as collateral damage from his parents' divorce.

All in all, I recommend this film to anyone interested in the subject of divorce. Alas, if only I could make it required viewing for everyone going through divorce!

9 ESSENTIAL TIPS FOR HELPING YOUR KIDS LONG TERM

1. Respect your child's feelings no matter what they are.
2. Don't argue with your ex in front of the kids, ever. This includes phone calls.
3. Never badmouth your ex to anyone in front of your kids or permit your family members or friends to do so.
4. Do not ask your child to take sides or allow your child to think that this is what you want.
5. Understand the importance of giving your child privacy. For example, a room that is a safe sanctuary.
6. Understand the importance of your child's social network. For example, your child's pet or your child's favorite objects.
7. Do not use your child as a messenger to the other parent.
8. Continue to seek the advice of experts on how to help your child.
9. Maintain these rules even after your child has reached adulthood.

MEDIATION, THE QUEEN OF A PEACEFUL DIVORCE

Why the "queen" of divorce? Because I firmly believe, compared to the warfare of litigation and the drawn-out bickering of intermediary lawyers, that mediation is the sanest, healthiest, fastest, least expensive, and least damaging way to dissolve a failed marriage and move forward into a new life.

Even now, several decades after mediation first made its way into family law, many people seem not to know about it or to have only a confused notion of what it might be. Some people assume that divorce mediation is the same thing as marriage counseling, with the goal of reconciling and remaining married. Of course, it is not: divorce mediation is a process for securing a divorce. If the couple signals that their goal is to remain married, the mediator suspends the mediation and refers them to marital counseling. Different professionals, different disciplines.

Some people assume that divorce mediation is a kind of arbitration in which the mediator hears both sides and then makes all the decisions, like a judge, only not in a courtroom and without the assistance of lawyers. This is completely wrong, of course: the mediator does not make any of the decisions.

Some people assume that the word mediation implies some kind of middle of the road divorce—perhaps like a highway median—that avoids the extremes of either staying in a terrible marriage or engaging in a lacerating winner versus loser pitched battle in a courtroom. In that they are not wrong, although that is not what mediation means. Mediation is about the middle, but that middle space is occupied by a neutral third party, the mediator, who helps both sides come to agreement on issues that had divided them. In fact, there are many uses for mediation in family law matters other than divorce, such as helping parties come to agreement on the care of an aging relative, or the transfer of child-rearing responsibilities to the grandparents, or in negotiating a complicated adoption. Divorce mediation is similar to these but applied to the acute crisis of a crumbling marital bond. Yet this cheaper, saner alternative is still unknown to many.

At one time I could have included myself in that same category. I didn't start out my legal career in family law; I started as a corporate lawyer working for a Fortune 500 company on their litigation team. The corporate world is full of disputes that lawyers try to resolve first through written communication, then by formal requests of record, and then by turning to the courts.

I remember the day things finally came to a head for me. I'd been working on a lawsuit against a vendor who provided our company with products that were essential to our own daily production. The vendor had been routinely late in getting the products to us, which in turn made us late rendering our services to clients. My boss was from the old school of lawyers whose approach to every problem was to annihilate the opposition. But I approached him looking for an alternative. I reminded him that such a severe action could lead the vendor to refuse to sell to us in the future, which would be disastrous. He didn't care. He replied in his usual way, punching the air with his fist while crying, "Crush the enemy!" It seemed more important to him to win than for our company to survive. My gut told me there had to be a better way to handle disputes between companies that were dependent on one another.

My observation as a young lawyer had been that the side with the most money seemed to win most of the time: The legal fight would go on until one side ran out of money and then the case would settle. Since the company I worked for had a lot of money, we usually won in court. I remember thinking this was not the way things should work in our legal system but had no idea what I could possibly do to change it.

Then, one day at lunch I overheard some attorneys talking about "alternative dispute resolution." I had never heard the term. With a little research, I soon learned that this method had been around for a long time; unions had been using it to negotiate with management, auto insurance companies had been using it to settle with injured parties, and Canadians had been using it to resolve issues with divorcing spouses. I couldn't wait to learn more. Since this was pre-Internet, I grabbed a copy of the yellow pages. Eventually I found a company called US Arbitration and Mediation, made a cold call, asked to speak with a mediator, and to my surprise, was put right through to a real, live person. He kindly made time to answer my many questions. Then I really hit the jackpot: When I asked to observe him mediating a case, he said yes. After one day of shadowing him and watching how he helped opposing parties resolve disputes in a respectful way, I was hooked. I went back to my bosses and tried to share this valuable approach, but no one was interested. (Many years later, the corporate world would widely adopt mediation to solve problems, but I was ahead of my time.)

I realized that if I were going to use my law degree to help resolve disputes through mediation, it was not going to be with my Fortune 500 employer. Much to the shock of my colleagues, friends, and family, I quit my cushy job. After taking courses, reading books, and talking to working mediators in various fields, I looked for a law firm with a mediation department. There was no such thing. So, I struck out on my own. To sustain myself, I taught law classes as adjunct faculty at a local university, and I started telling everyone I knew about mediation. Slowly but surely I acquired clients for family mediation, largely through referrals from marriage counselors whose clients had ultimately decided to divorce. It was a perfect fit.

For one thing, divorce mediation was simply a better fit for my personality than the ferociously combative corporate world I'd experienced. For another, I found in it the promise of the kind of gratification I'd been seeking: the possibility of truly helping people. A gifted mediator can help families avoid the most damaging aspects of divorce. Children will still need co-parenting after the divorce; a mediator helps the divorcing couple work together on how best to accomplish that. By the time the mediation is done, both parents have agreed on the structure of the co-parenting arrangement and, it is hoped, learned how to behave so that they can avoid conflict and successfully co-parent. The difference between this kind of mediation and what I'd experienced in corporate law couldn't have been clearer.

Eventually, I decided I could be even more effective if I acquired more insight into the interactions of spouses. I attended the Menninger Institute for Marriage and Family Counseling for two years. I did not want to become a marriage counselor, but after a friend pointed out that, in a sense, what I was doing amounted to "divorce counseling," a graduate degree in counseling seemed logical. That was many years ago, and I still use that counseling education in my practice every day. Law and counseling turned out to be an ideal combination for helping couples divorce respectfully through mediation.

NOT ALL MEDIATION IS THE SAME

The kind of civil mediation used by corporations in conflict is called positional bargaining. The clients and their attorneys are in different rooms, and the mediator shuttles back and forth between them, trying to maneuver them into a "zone of agreement." In my experience, the reality of this is a good deal more combative than it sounds. By contrast, in family law we practice what's called interest-based mediation, so named because we try to help both parties arrive at an agreement that, to the greatest extent possible, serves the best interests of both parties. In a divorce mediation, there are no teams of lawyers, just the divorcing couple and the mediator. The mediator always meets with both spouses together, so everything is open and all information shared. The mediator is impartial and serves as a guide to help the couple arrive at an agreement regarding property division, maintenance, and the co-parenting of their children. The atmosphere can at times be tense, but any attempts at introducing conflict—verbal or physical—are immediately shut down by the mediator.

The whole process is geared toward finding the win-win solution for both parties and their children. The resulting agreement, which will be reviewed by a judge for fairness, is the product of trades and compromises made by the spouses so that they each get what they need to lead their separate lives—or, as I put it to my clients, what they will need to want to wake up in the morning and live their new lives. Divorce doesn't mean their lives are ending. It isn't just destruction and dismantling. Mediation gets the divorcing spouses to realize this by having them think beyond their current misery to collaborate on a plan that provides the best possible future for all. At its heart, it's about hope and cooperation, with a good measure of creativity thrown in.

When I set out to become a family law mediator, I trained with four different mediators to learn about the different styles of communication, observe their mediating process and the way they handled their clients, and find a style I wished to emulate. It was a helpful experience, because I saw how much mediators differ from one another. It was the early days for family law mediation in the United States (it began in Canada decades earlier) and the first mediators inevitably put their own stamp on this growing field with their personal styles. Eventually, the styles became so distinct that they acquired names. There are several principal styles and all are acceptable; most mediators use a combination of these different types and switch among them depending on what they believe might be most effective in a specific situation and for that particular couple.

It is helpful for anyone considering divorce mediation to know about these styles, so you can make an informed choice about the mediator you pick. Make a list of divorce mediators in your area and read their websites to gain insight into the kind of mediation they use. Then call and ask for a fifteen-minute informational interview. Ask about the style when you meet the mediator. Here are brief descriptions of three of the most commonly used styles.

1. **Facilitative mediation.** This happened to be the first kind I studied, because the training course was offered right at the time I was looking for one. The mediator was a civil mediator who worked in corporate mediation, but he was offering a course for family law mediators. The style he practiced was one in which he stepped back and allowed the two opposing parties to set the agenda and then talk—or yell—at each other. He saw his role as enabling the two sides to have a dialogue and come up with a way to resolve their issue. He interfered as little as possible, only working to keep the interaction civil, to provide information and suggestions when they became stuck, and take notes for what would be the ultimate agreement. Because the facilitative mediator is not directing every detail of the process, it takes a long time, typically around a dozen sessions, to arrive at an agreement covering all points.

2. **Highly directive mediation.** This would be the opposite of facilitative, because the mediator is very controlling of every aspect of the process. This kind of mediator might give people directions and use drama to get points across. This might be a good choice for couples who are very combative and need to be controlled. When I first established my practice in St. Louis, there was only one other mediator in town, and to say he practiced highly directive mediation would be an understatement. He was known to have angry outbursts in

front of his clients, throw chairs, flip over tables. He also had a pair of intimidating Doberman pinschers who were allowed to move around freely in the room where the mediation was taking place. One couple he was working with fired him and hired me to finish their mediation process; the wife told me that one day she made the mistake of wearing sandals to the mediation session and the dogs got under the table and nipped at her toes. This highly directive mediator later moved to the West Coast, where he remains very popular. My point in relaying this story is that you need to select the kind of mediator you will be most comfortable with.

3. **Transformative mediation.** The style known as transformative mediation aims at a goal that is higher than the immediate objective of dissolving the marriage. It is also a teaching process: First, to give both parties hope for a brighter future and the confidence to move toward it. Second, it educates both parties in how to discuss and resolve any future issue of co-parenting in a civil and productive manner, lessening stress for all concerned and allowing their children to thrive in the new, conflict-free situation. This is the style I practice, although I integrate elements of many other styles, as needed. Many couples tell me that if they'd understood much earlier how to work out their differences in a calm, respectful way, their marriage likely would not have deteriorated to the point of divorce. One couple whose divorce I mediated wrote me about a year later to tell me that what they learned in mediation transformed their relationship so much that they eventually decided to remarry each other. That was a lovely, gratifying thing to hear. But just to be clear, the point of transformational divorce mediation is not to make everything hunky-dory and get the couple to reaffirm their marriage. That's the job of marriage counselors, not mediators. Every couple's situation is unique and there are many, many reasons couples decide to divorce. Marriages fail; divorce happens. Transformational mediation came about in

order to help couples who find themselves in that situation come to an agreement on how to dissolve their marriage in the least damaging way possible, while learning the skills they will need to co-parent successfully in their post-divorce lives. It is the polar opposite of scorched-earth legal warfare, although I grant that there is a need for that, as well, in the world of divorce.

Clearly, my point of view is that, where possible, mediation is the very best way to get divorced: better for the kids, better for the emotional health of the parents, better for the pocketbook. It is increasingly common, but there are still many unhappy couples who have never heard about it. Why not? Perhaps this is because mediated divorces don't make for great TV or movies. (Who would pay to see *The Non-War of the Roses?*) Perhaps it's because many of my brother and sister lawyers don't steer clients in the direction of mediation when there is more money to be made in legal warfare. And perhaps it's mainly because the practice of mediation is still relatively new.

The entire field is fairly new, although in northern Europe it became widely accepted decades ago. In Norway, for instance, mediation has been compulsory since 1993 for couples with children younger than sixteen, except in cases involving domestic violence.[5] In the United Kingdom, mediation, called "conciliation" there, has been around since the 1970s. In Sweden, 90 percent of divorcing couples are divorced through "cooperation talks," their term for mediation. In some European countries, particularly Eastern and Southern Europe, mediation is still rare.

It may be no accident that the person primarily responsible for bringing mediation to family law in the United States was actually British. John M. Haynes (1932–99), who emigrated to the United States when he was twenty-five years old, earned his PhD in social policy at Union College in New York, and became a mediator,

---

[5] Miguel Martin Casals, *Divorce Mediation in Europe: An Introductory Outline*, Electronic Journal of Comparative Law, vol. 9.2 (July 2005), 7, < http:/ /www.ejcl.org / >, 8.

spending much of his career working for a labor union. His career unfolded against a backdrop of rising divorce in the states, and this caught his attention. Although he was a positional bargaining mediator in the world of labor relations, he could see the need for mediation in divorces in the United States and he was very much aware of how interest-based mediation (or conciliation) was being used in the United Kingdom. Haynes turned his attention to developing the kind of mediation that could potentially bring easier, less stressful, and even healing solutions to divorcing couples.

I studied with John Haynes and nearly memorized his 1981 book, *Divorce Mediation: A Practical Guide for Therapists and Counselors*. The Haynes style of mediation—gentle, yet firm—was the style I wanted to emulate. He was soft spoken and respectful to everyone. I thought: *That's the kind of mediator I want to be. It suits my personality. I'm not controlling, and I don't throw chairs.* A mediator needs to have a style that authentically reflects her personality or the clients won't believe her.

I also learned a lot from Haynes's instructional videotapes. He taped several actual divorce mediations with the consent of the couples. He did not charge them for his mediation if they signed a waiver allowing him to capture the sessions on film. (This probably could not have been done in the United States, even back in the 1980s, but he did this in Canada where the privacy laws were different.)

Haynes's sessions began with three chairs in a triangle formation. He did not use a table for the negotiations, because he felt it was a barrier between himself and the clients. During a session shown on one of his tapes, the couple shouted at one another, which can be dangerous. Divorcing couples know how to push each other's buttons, and the situation can escalate rapidly. Haynes calmed them down quickly, not by shouting or threatening them, but by standing up and placing himself between them, speaking softy and reframing their words at how he thought each was feeling and asking for confirmation. It was brilliant and immediately deescalated the situation.

Haynes's approach to mediating divorce got the attention of mediators and lawyers across the country, and it caught on. He taught that it is extremely important for the mediator to be able to quickly and accurately identify what the key issues are for each person; the degree in which each parent is invested and committed to the responsibilities of child rearing; what each spouse's hopes are for the independent life to come; and where spouses might be deceiving themselves. In order to do an effective job, the mediator must learn a great deal about the clients, including confidential information. These are not unnecessary intrusions into the private lives and hidden desires of clients struggling through the unraveling of a marriage. The more the mediator understands about the individual personalities and family dynamics of the clients, the better the chances of guiding them to an agreement. Insights are the building blocks for a mediator's strategy, and every divorce mediation requires a specially tailored strategy. What does this husband really want? What does this wife really need? What might be a bargaining chip? A highly skilled mediator has a whole toolkit of ways to gain insight into what really counts for each spouse and what sorts of tradeoffs might be feasible.

Before I sit down for the first mediation session with a couple, I have each complete a form with biographical information and write out their goals for themselves and their children. I have them each make a drawing of his or her most desired post-divorce future. I ask them to put into the drawing what they will need that will give them a reason to get up in the morning. This is very similar to the technique I mentioned in chapter 1, when a client is trying to figure out whether to divorce. In both types of situations, the drawing helps the clients attain some clarity, because drawing forces them to figure out their priorities and helps them break through subconscious shoulds and should nots that can interfere with their ability to break through to their real goals.

Such drawings have proved incredibly revealing and help me get right to what matters most to each party. They show me the emotional truths of the situation faster than anything else and clue me in as to how to weigh the veracity of what the spouses say during the mediation session. In my experience, people who come in to get a divorce, whether through mediation or litigation, very often say things that aren't true. There are many reasons people do this. Maybe it's about covering up some misdeed or hiding assets from the spouse. Or maybe they are having trouble facing something and are lying about it as much to themselves as to me. Sometimes at the outset they claim to want a particular thing or outcome, which they know the other spouse wants desperately, when the real motivation is simply to anger the spouse or cause worry or inconvenience. This is just human nature, and when couples divorce, the best side of their natures is not usually the one on display. Because divorce is such a huge and painful crisis and generates enormous stress, it's hard for people to behave well and even harder for them to think clearly about what they truly need and what they are willing to give up. I'll give some examples of how a client's drawing helps me cut to the chase.

THE CASE OF PALM TREE MAN

A husband came in wanting a divorce. He said he really wanted his kids and to split everything, including custody, equally with his wife. To my surprise, the picture he drew of his future life showed a cruise ship headed toward an island with one palm tree and a figure of himself relaxing under it, sitting in a beach chair, holding a drink with a little umbrella in it. Unfortunately, I cannot share these drawings with you in this book because it could violate attorney-client privilege if someone recognized a specific person from his or her drawing.

"Are the kids on the cruise ship?" I asked.

He said no.

"Are they on the island with the palm tree?"

No again.

We talked some more. Finally, he confessed. "My whole family will think I'm a loser if I don't get 50/50 custody of the kids." But what he really wanted was to retire early and sit on this island. The children weren't all that important.

This knowledge was crucial for me to help him design a future life that he wanted to wake up to. After reminding him that *he* was designing his own life, not the life others though he should live, he was able to follow his own truth and create a retirement future that reflected *his* goal, not worrying about what other people thought he should do.

In comparing his drawing with his wife's, it was clear there need be no battle over custody of the children. Her's depicted her life revolving around the children and their activities, school, sports, family, vacations, pets, church, etc. This couple could have spent thousands of dollars and several years fighting over custody of the children, when clearly, that was not an issue for them. Dad's honesty in his drawing of his ideal future prevented wasteful fighting over the children, and this case settled quickly in mediation, with each party getting what they really wanted with the least amount of fighting and expense.

THE WOMAN WHO LIKED POOL BOYS

Midway through my career, I worked with a couple who wisely chose the mediation process to come to an agreement regarding the division of their assets and parenting responsibilities. They had been married for more than twenty years, during which three children were born into their family. Dad was the sole breadwinner, and Mom stayed home with the children. They were able to afford a large, comfortable home with a pool. Dad worked long hours to earn the family's fortune and had to travel extensively. Left alone to raise the children while her husband was away, Mom got lonely. She had a series of affairs with handymen and pool boys. Each affair was with a young man about half her age. I don't know the specifics of how or when her husband found out, but after she admitted the infidelity, they sought marriage counseling together. Although she understood the havoc her unfaithfulness had on the entire family, she found it difficult to stop this pattern of behavior. Although her husband was a kind, attractive, successful businessman, she was continually drawn to younger men.

This couple owned a vacation home in California right on the beach. They had a trial separation, during which she went to the beach house to live for a few months, while the dad cared for the children in the marital residence. Mom soon struck up a relationship with her young karate instructor and another affair began. That was the last straw for Dad, and he made an appointment with me to resolve the issues of their divorce using mediation.

I had each of them draw a picture of their wished-for future. Not yet knowing all the information explained above, I was slightly surprised at each party's picture of their ideal future.

Mom had drawn a scene of "fun in the sun" at their beach house with palm trees, a sailboat, time for karate, of course, and a symbol of a 9-5 job with a slash through it, indicating that she did not want to have to work outside the home. The most telling part of her picture was that all the fun things in her life took up about 95 percent of the picture. Her three children occupied a small triangle at the bottom of the page in the right-hand corner. They seemed so small compared to the rest of the life she wanted.

Dad's picture was quite the opposite. He drew the marital residence in the middle of the page. Then he drew several circles of things he felt were important to keep in his life post-divorce. He drew himself with the three children, time with the extended family, kids' sports, school, college, church, and the children's pets.

Dad was extremely generous in the division of property, offering Mom more than fifty percent of the assets, because, as explained with tears in his eyes, this divorce was not about punishment or revenge. Rather, it was a way for her to live the life she wanted without shame or guilt and the best way to reduce conflict between them.

He offered her more money in maintenance than she asked for and offered to pay for one round-trip flight from California back to the marital residence once a month to see the children for as long as she wanted. He even offered to pay for an apartment for her near the marital residence so she would have a private place to spend time with the children when she came back to visit.

Interestingly, they had one very important family event on the near horizon that needed some attention: a child's departure for college. Despite the tears, apologies, forgiveness, and understanding that took place during this couple's mediation, the children still felt the discord in their parents' marriage. Consequently, when discussing the specifics around the oldest child's departure for college, Dad said the child had made one request: that he not have to ride in the car with both parents. He felt the tension between them and didn't want to experience that awkwardness for the two-day drive to the university. He didn't care who he rode with but asked that one parent drive him down and the other parent visit the next weekend.

Fortunately, these parents honored their child's boundaries and agreed to the following sequence of events. Dad drove him to college, helped him move into his dorm, took him to dinner and left. The next weekend, Mom came for a visit, took him shopping and to dinner, and then left. What a smart kid! He got to experience the best each parent had to offer with no fighting or awkward silence in the long car ride. And kudos to these parents for honoring their child's wishes. It took a one-hour mediation session for Mom and Dad to agree to these arrangements, but it was well worth it. This was their first "mediated argument," wherein their focus was on honoring the needs and expressed boundaries of their child. My hope for them is that this was the first of many such compromises this couple agreed to in their attempt to put the children's needs first.

THE STORY OF LOG CABIN MAN

A couple came in for mediation. They'd been married a long time and had several children. Each said they wanted custody. The husband's picture of his ideal future was very detailed. It showed a log cabin in the woods with smoke coming out of the chimney, with lots of trees around it and a long gravel road leading up to it. He drew himself inside the cabin, seated in a chair in front of a table with an open laptop. On the floor next to him was a case of beer. No children were in the picture. The wife's picture showed a home and kids in the center of the page. Everything revolved around the kids. She drew lines out to show her volunteer work at the school, their church activities, her attendance at their sports events, and time for her children to be with their friends.

When in the course of the mediation we arrived at the subject of child custody, the husband again said he wanted custody split 50/50.

"But you don't do anything with the kids," his wife said. "Our son is a star basketball player, and you don't even go to his games! If you're so interested in participating in the kids' lives, why aren't you doing any of it now?" She angrily added that he was addicted to alcohol and Internet porn.

He simply said, "Our lives are very different, and that is why we are getting a divorce."

After more discussion about each party's goals, the dad admitted that his idea behind asking for 50/50 custody was his belief that under such an arrangement, he would not have to pay his wife any child support. Of course, this was completely wrong. I explained that he was going to pay child support no matter what. He could have 80 percent custody and would still pay child support. He was the sole earner, and his wife, who has stayed home for the last twenty years, needed a house big enough for the children and enough money to maintain the house and pay for their needs. Since his custody request was obviously a smokescreen and the real issue for him was money, I saw that I shouldn't spend a lot of time on custody and should instead focus on how the children would be financially supported.

In Missouri, at the time of writing this book, you could get a discount on the amount of child support you pay proportionate to the amount of time you say you are going to spend with the kids. If this husband had received 50/50 custody but didn't really take responsibility for them for half the time, his wife and kids would have been financially devastated. She needed a minimum of $2,000 a month for the kids, but with a 50/50 custody plan she would have gotten only half that amount, even though he had little or no interest in ever exercising his child custody arrangement, and she would have been caring for the kids nearly 100 percent of the time. Instead, we worked out a child support and spousal maintenance arrangement in which he paid a combined sum per month to his former wife and did not have to take on any of the day-to-day costs of the care of the children. And he did get himself a log cabin in the woods.

This was a case where the drawing he made for me about his desired future was accurate, but what he had said verbally during mediation sessions was not. He just couldn't bring himself to tell me what he really wanted, which was to go live by himself in the woods and be left alone by everybody, including his kids. The agreement we eventually worked out was respectful of everyone's needs. It was fortunate that this couple worked out their divorce through mediation rather than litigation. If the case had been tried in court, a judge might well have granted 50/50 custody of the children, since that is what the statutes suggest in the jurisdictions in which I practice. It would have resulted in the mother having terrible financial problems and the kids spending substantial time with a parent who didn't really want them around.

A good mediator isn't out to judge anyone, punish anyone, improve anyone's character, heal anyone's emotional wounds, or change anyone's priorities. A good mediator meets the clients where they are and cuts through the emotional noise to help them look forward in hope, not backward in guilt and recrimination. The skill is in guiding the couple to an agreement that truly meets each spouse's needs and those of the kids and is sustainable, even if it differs from what each spouse initially claimed.

When I watched John Haynes at work in a mediation, I could see that he transformed the way people argued. I already knew, from reading a book by Judith Wallerstein, the mental health professional mentioned earlier in this book who studied the impact of divorce on children, that it is not the divorce per se that damages children; it is the open conflict between the parents that is witnessed by the children. Putting these two rich sources of wisdom together, I felt that for most couples headed for divorce, transformative mediation was the answer. Couples on their way to divorce need to learn how to resolve disagreements with one another in a way that defuses anger rather than escalating it. That way they can co-parent into the future in a way that addresses problems with the intent of finding a solution together rather than seizing upon each disagreement as an opportunity to trade accusations and insults.

Typically, when couples argue, it takes the form of blaming, criticizing, or catastrophizing. The statements tend to be absolute or exaggerated rather than tempered or realistic. "You never unload the dishwasher!" "You never help with the kids' homework!" "You always spend too much money on clothes!" "You always play golf with your buddies every Saturday, and I'm stuck with all the chores!" "You never appreciate how hard I work to support you and the kids!" It's about what the other person does or doesn't do, and it's phrased in an absolute way that slams the door on constructive discussion. That kind of blanket accusation ignores the times the other person actually did help in those or other ways and implies that the aggrieved spouse is taking every failing as an intentional act of insult or neglect. No wonder both wind up feeling defensive and furious.

Whether the person shirks the chores or spends more money than his or her partner is not really the issue; the issue is always bigger and stands in the background, obscured by the scaffolding of innumerable accusations concerning the minutiae of daily family life. For example, the issue might well be something like, "I need help!" or "I do a lot, and I need you to acknowledge that and tell me how much you appreciate it." I hear this and think: *Is the bigger issue that she wants more assistance or that she wants him to clearly appreciate her efforts?*

When I get a sense of what the background issue may be, I test my hypothesis with a question that will try to rephrase it using different words and in a broader, more inclusive way. I'll say, "So, Jill, let me see if I understand this correctly. Are you feeling that Jack needs to take over the dishwasher chore or is it something bigger? Okay, it's bigger. Are you saying you want him to take note of all you do for the family and openly validate that contribution, even though what you do doesn't feed the bank account?"

Sometimes I am right in my hypothesis, and sometimes Jill will correct me: "No! I'm saying that he is incapable of taking care of the kids, and I'm worried about how they will fare if he has custody half the time."

Whether my interpretation was right or wrong, the discussion has been transformed; now we are talking about the bigger issue. We've gotten away from the spouses trading accusations, and we're working together to get at the core problem. And Jill is getting better and better at clearly stating what she needs. Bit by bit Jill's real issue comes into focus. She wants Jack to see the kids and have a relationship with them, but she is afraid that when the kids are with him they won't receive the care they need. They'll get McDonald's meals for breakfast, lunch, and dinner. He won't get them to bed on time. He won't give them a bath. She is the one who has taken care of the kids' needs and kept the house clean. She has no evidence that Jack can do these things and has not heard what she needs to hear from Jack in order to calm her concerns. That's when I will lay out several options for how to address Jill's concern. Would hiring a nanny or a housekeeper a couple of days a week help? Would it help to have nutritious meals delivered and to eat off of paper plates to avoid a sink full of dirty dishes?

Sometimes the other spouse will react to the accusations by saying Jill shouldn't feel what she says she is feeling. A good mediator shuts that down right away: "We are not here to pass judgment on how Jill feels. The fact is, she does feel that way, so what can you decide together that will resolve this concern?"

Sometimes I have the spouse practice rephrasing the concern and then adopting a positive, solution-oriented attitude: "Okay, Jill, you feel like that. I don't think you should, but you do. So, let's brainstorm how to make Jill feel better. My goal is for you to not feel trapped."

If a couple comes back three or four times, they have usually learned the new way of airing concerns and addressing them and are doing it on their own.

Earlier, I mentioned a couple who mediated their divorce and later wound up remarrying one another. They had a style of fighting that revolved around blame and defensiveness. This kind of fighting would also start an argument about X when really the problem was Z. Later, when this couple wrote to say they'd remarried, they said that in mediation they'd learned how to find out the real underlying problem rather than blaming the other party. "We ask each other questions now and then we brainstorm about how to resolve the problem." It was critical for them to learn how to ask each other questions in a nondefamatory way and to recognize and respect what the other person was feeling.

Before, when the husband, for example, spoke of his pain about something, the wife would typically protest, "But he shouldn't feel like that!"

I would tell her, "No one has the right to tell another person how he should feel. If he says that's how he feels, then that's how he feels. We are not here to judge him. Our job is to figure out what needs to change so he no longer feels this way. Let's start brainstorming options that might help him feel differently. Can you come up with an option we can put on the table for discussion? And then maybe he can suggest an option that he thinks could help."

One of my favorite phrases I learned from my mentor is, "I'm not here to help you rehash the past; I'm here to help you reshape your future." It works like a charm!

This couple had been to marriage counseling but didn't learn these techniques there. While many marriage counselors do specifically teach technique, their particular counselor may have used a more esoteric model, while what I taught them was practical. One methodology is not better than the other; they are just different. After their divorce, they continued to use the methods they'd learned in mediation as they co-parented their two kids. As time passed, it became fully integrated into their manner of relating to one another; they'd gotten practice while working together on the kids' issues, and then they learned how to handle their own. One day they told me they asked each other, "Why are we divorced? We work so well together now." And they remarried each other.

It's unusual for a divorced couple to remarry, but the story serves to illustrate a huge benefit of mediation. The process naturally elevates the couple's interactions, because it changes the point of departure for every discussion. Instead of squaring off in opposition, the couple, guided by the mediator, find themselves on the same team, working to solve problems that affect both their lives. They've constructed a new platform on which both can stand, equal in stature, and it is now possible to communicate without acrimony and resolve parenting issues in a collaborative manner. If both spouses take the lessons of mediation to heart, the result is a divorce agreement they have worked together to create and that they know they can sustain. As they go forward post-divorce into their separate lives—but still co-parenting—the stress level will be a lot lower for them and their kids.

Another example of the great potential benefit of mediation concerns the case of an executive and his wife, a social worker. Following an accident, the husband had become addicted to painkillers and his marriage fell apart. He successfully went through chemical dependency rehab and was even able to keep his job, but the divorce went forward anyway. He was devastated at the prospect, because he was still in love with his wife and adored their child, who was just about to enter primary school. Fortunately, both spouses were willing to mediate, which kept the matter totally private instead of exposing it in the courtroom. They were able to work out an agreement in which the wife and child could stay in the marital home and the parents shared custody. Their communication with one another had also benefited from what they learned in the mediation process.

About six months after the divorce, I ran into the father at a store. He came up to me with his child in tow, hugged me, and started to cry. He thanked me for mediating his divorce, because it helped them make the decisions they wanted to keep the conflict low. He and his ex-wife had been able to be in the same room without difficulty. He was especially grateful that his ex-wife included him in Christmas at her house, even though according to the plan she had sole custody that weekend. He cried again as he told me how much it meant to him to spend Christmas with his child and around his former wife, whom he still loved, in the marital residence he had built. I told him not to thank me but to thank the process of mediation, because it was that process that kept them in control of the decision making and educated them in how to avoid conflict and remain friends.

I don't want to leave the impression that mediation is for everyone. There are plenty of couples who cannot or should not try it. The three biggest barriers to using mediation to divorce are (1) physical abuse, (2) substance addiction, and (3) mental illness. The process cannot function as intended if one spouse intimidates the other through abuse or if there are conditions that interfere with rational thought.

Here are some other categories where mediation would not be wise:

1. **If either party is constitutionally ill-suited to the mediation process.** The longest mediation case I ever had lasted thirteen sessions because the wife was incapable of making a decision and sticking with it. (She was working on this issue with a psychiatrist at the same time she and her husband were mediating.) She would agree to a number of items during a mediation session but change her mind at the door on her way out. So, at the next mediation session we had to start back at ground zero. She wasn't mentally ill. She just didn't have the self-confidence to make a decision and then stick with it. I made sure she had a good lawyer to run all her decisions by, and she continued working with her psychiatrist during this process. This couple was able to finally come to an agreement with the help of these outside parties.

2. **If either party is an extreme narcissist.** Such spouses only care about themselves. They lack the compassion to care about the spouse's or children's needs. So when it comes to exploring options that could alleviate the spouse's concerns, one of the core components of mediation, the narcissist fails miserably. Instead of looking for solutions to the problem, he or she often refuses to acknowledge the problem and demeans the spouse for even thinking it. Then he or she tries to redirect the discussion to something else, trying to dismiss the concern with phrases such as, "Oh, it's stupid to worry about that." "That will never happen, trust me. I know better than you." Or he or she will respond by demeaning or shutting down the spouse: "I can't believe you're still worried about that! What's wrong with you? You are so irrational, I swear, I don't know how you get through the day without me there directing you on how to do every little thing!"

It takes a skilled mediator to turn this type of manipulation around. Through years of advanced training in techniques to defuse anger between spouses, I've learned to turn the discussion right back to the narcissist's behavior. I remind him or her of the rules of mediation I initially gave them, in which each spouse gets to express any concern, and it is the responsibility of all three of us (mediator and both spouses) to put our heads together and figure out how to solve it. "So stop telling your spouse not to worry. Your spouse has the right to worry about whatever may be a concern. It's our job to address that concern so that it is no longer a source of worry." I have had many people write to me after I mediated their divorce telling me what an impact it had when I made the narcissistic spouse stop demeaning the spouse at the mediation table. One woman wrote to me that I was the first person who'd ever told her husband that he couldn't talk to her that way. No one had ever stood up for her concerns and made her husband try to resolve the issue instead of calling her stupid and shrugging it off.

3. **If either party is very controlling or threatening.** Once a police officer and his wife came to me to mediate their divorce. At the first meeting, the officer was in full uniform, which I thought was very strange. He refused to sit at the table. Instead, he stood and put some type of document in the middle of the table, retrieved his service revolver, laid it on top of the document, and proclaimed; "I'm ready to mediate; all I need is my wife's signature on these documents."

I had a kneejerk reaction to seeing his gun on my conference table. I instinctively retorted, "No, sir. I think you're ready to intimidate, not mediate. Please sit down." He refused. It's only fair to disclose that this was the closest I had ever been to a gun in my life, so my reaction may have been a little overkill. But I reached for the gun, touching one of these cold, black, metal, scary things for the first time in my life. I slowly slid the gun off the table and onto my lap, out of his reach. I called for my secretary, who immediately entered the room, and asked her to call building security to have a guard walk the husband to his car. She did, but he said he was not leaving without his service weapon.

At this point I asked him which police precinct he worked for. He gave me a number. Then the security guard for my twenty-three-story office building, who is not allowed to carry a gun, entered the conference room. Now, this husband was in his late thirties, about six feet tall, about 250 pounds, and very muscular. Our security guard, on the other hand, was about seventy-five years old, 170 pounds wet, and slightly crippled over with a cane. I almost laughed at the thought of what a rumble between this husband and our security guard would look like—smackdown in five seconds flat in the cop's favor.

Surprisingly, when the security guard asked the husband to follow him, the husband followed him! On his way out, he yelled back over his shoulder, "Hey, what about my gun?" I answered, "You can pick it up from your precinct tomorrow." And out the door they walked. My secretary ran to the door of our office and locked it. My immediate thought was, *Big help that deadbolt on the door is.* The door was entirely plate glass, and the husband could have gained reentry with a mere kick of one boot. But luckily, he left.

I gently lifted the gun back onto the table, still afraid it could accidently discharge. I called the husband's police precinct and asked to talk to his superior. I vaguely explained that the husband had left his police revolver at my office and asked if they would like for me to return it to the station. They seemed more distressed than I was and said they would immediately send over two officers to get the gun. I asked for them to send a third officer to escort wife home safely. Of course, they agreed and sent over two squad cars in a flash.

I explained to the wife that I could not discuss what happened because of mediator confidentiality, but she could say anything she wanted. Finally, I told her not to return to mediation as this process clearly was not the best process for them. There can be no intimidation or threats in mediation. Mediation, by definition, is "self-determination," not fear induced. She acknowledged my comments and left with the police escort. That's where the story ends. I have no idea what happened to either of them after that day in my office.

I learned something valuable: I needed to get more comfortable around firearms if I was going to stay in this line of work. Subsequently, a friend of mine who used to be a police officer has taken me to the shooting range to introduce me to shooting. Learning how to make sure the safety latch is on, understanding how to target shoot, and getting used to the sound of a gun shooting was very helpful. It was important to get over my fear of guns in case anyone else ever brings one along to a mediation session ... you know ... just because it might "help" the spouse be a little more cooperative.

4. **If either party is a pathological liar.** Sometimes one spouse is convinced the other spouse will lie when requested to disclose assets. In one case, a woman who was an independent landscaper was usually paid in cash for her work. She kept all the money in a safe deposit box. She didn't want to pay taxes on her earnings, so she did everything in cash. Her spouse was afraid she would not fully disclose her earnings in an attempt to give him less than 50 percent of the marital assets. He was convinced she would lie about her income.

If your spouse is a liar, and you think he or she is going to lie about and hide money, then mediation may not be the best method of divorce for you. It may be that you have no other option than to litigate. One of the benefits of litigation is that your lawyer can conduct what is called discovery, in which the lawyer can demand records showing income, withdrawals, expenditures, investments, and the like. For example, the attorney can

a. *subpoena* records from a bank to see if large amounts of money were deposited or withdrawn from an account with only your spouse's name on it;

b. send *requests for production of documents* to your spouse, requiring him or her to turn over certain records;

c. send your spouse *interrogatories*, which are written questions about his or her finances, for example, that the spouse must answer thoroughly in writing and under oath;

d. *subpoena* your spouse for a deposition, in which your attorney can interrogate your spouse in front of a court reporter and your spouse will be required to answer questions under oath; or

e. issue other forms of discovery that are meant to uncover hidden information.

However, be aware that these methods are not foolproof. Just consider the last example in which the wife hid cash in a safe deposit box and was a liar. Not even formal discovery techniques can find everything if your spouse is an excellent liar.

If any of the above situations apply to you, and that short list is by no means exhaustive, you may want to go straight to litigation, which is the longer, more expensive, more contentious, and more stressful road—but perhaps the surest one. However, you'd better understand something first.

THE MOST IMPORTANT THING TO UNDERSTAND ABOUT LITIGATING YOUR DIVORCE

Taking your divorce to a courtroom battleground is one big, expensive gamble. You don't know which judge will be assigned to your case. You don't know the judge's sympathies, prejudices, emotional baggage, or state of mental or physical health. But that judge is going to make decisions that affect your life and the lives of your children for years. You are putting your fate in the hands of a total stranger.

I have known some excellent judges. But I have also seen judges decide cases in ways that defy belief, and you need to understand right now that there is no guarantee you will get a result that is remotely fair.

THE SEX ADDICT

I remember the case of a couple with two young kids in which the wife discovered by accident that her husband was a sex addict. He traveled a great deal for his job, so he found it easy to have sex with gay prostitutes and keep it all hidden from his wife. The situation was really over the top. He had infected her with STDs and HIV, although she didn't know any of that until after she stumbled upon his secret life. When she occasionally went on trips for her work, he brought prostitutes into the house at night—while the children were asleep down the hall. The family computer had been used so much for pornographic web surfing that graphic messages popped up on the screen, which is how the whole thing came to light. The wife was mortified, angry, and deeply worried about the kids. I felt sure we could get her sole custody of the children under these circumstances, since the dad had continually put the children at risk. After all, how could any judge not see the wisdom of keeping the kids out of the home of a sex addict who brought prostitute strangers home and left obscene material where kids could happen upon it? Despite all the evidence and despite the pleas of the guardian ad litem who'd been hired by the court to look into the matter and advise on what was best for the kids, the judge said he thought it wasn't a big deal and granted the parents 50/50 custody. I was aghast. My client was beside herself. The guardian ad litem was speechless.

In the end, my client and I worked out an agreement with Dad in which the kids would never spend the night at his house, even though the court had given him the right to have the children spend the night with him 50 percent of the time. The fact was, he didn't want the kids overnight, because it interfered with his private life. He'd asked for 50/50 custody so his child support payments would be less. But it was worth it to the kids' mother to receive less in child support if she could protect them from harm. The husband agreed to take the kids one afternoon a weekend and always on an outing to a public place, which is all he really wanted. It had turned into a mostly livable situation, but the horror of that case still reverberates with me after many years.

MY CLIENT WITH SEVERE PHYSICAL DISABILITIES

I represented a client who suffered from blindness and paraplegia and was confined to a wheelchair. His wife had filed for divorce. Wife had a good job earning more than $100,000 a year. They had no children during their twenty-year marriage. At our first settlement conference with the judge in this litigated case, I brought up the issue of maintenance for the husband. I explained the cost of home health care versus an institution to care for him. This was my first appearance in front of this particular judge. To my surprise, his response to my request for maintenance was, "No way." At least he was honest enough to explain his reasoning. He said he was paying maintenance to two ex-wives and was never going to saddle another person who appeared before him with maintenance. I reminded him that my client could not support himself due to his physical disabilities.

He said flippantly "Well, maybe he could get one of those Saturday morning TV shows where people paint with their feet."

I reminded him that he was *blind*, and even if he could paint with a brush between his toes, he could not *see* the canvas. But the judge seemed more focused on himself than the circumstances of my client. He repeated his vow of never saddling anyone with maintenance again because he was tired of paying his two exes. Fortunately, I was still within a window of time that I could file a request for a new judge, which is exactly what I did. We were assigned to a much more sympathetic judge who saw the need for financial support of my client. Another lesson I learned—if a client requesting maintenance got assigned to Judge No-Maintenance, I immediately filed a request for a new judge.

If you take these tips and cautionary tales to heart, I promise you that, at a minimum, your divorce experience will be a lot better than if you hadn't. In the best scenario, your spouse will act similarly and your case will settle quickly, the judge will sign off on it, and each of you will be free to move forward with rebuilding your separate lives. Admittedly though, a lot of things are out of your control.

The Sixth Secret

DOMESTIC VIOLENCE MAKES DIVORCE A WHOLE DIFFERENT EXPERIENCE

Perhaps you are considering divorce because you or others in your household are in danger or that threat hangs in the background. If so, you may have many questions about how raising the subject of domestic violence affects a divorce proceeding. You may also be wondering whether your spouse's actions, while frightening to you, rise to the level of a legal definition of domestic violence. So let's make sure you are clear about the kinds of actions that constitute domestic violence and how such actions can impact your divorce proceedings.

Domestic violence is a pattern of assaultive and coercive behaviors that adults or adolescents use against their current or former intimate partners.[6] Notice that this definition does not require black eyes, bruises, broken bones, marks, scratches, or any physical harm. Rather, it is a pattern of behavior used by your intimate partner to control you. It could include such things as coercion ("It's your

---

[6] I like this definition, which is from the Missouri Coalition against Domestic and Sexual Violence.

duty to have sex with me when I want it. You don't want to be a bad spouse, do you?"), manipulation ("If you stay away from your friend Chris, who badmouths me, I'll get you that thing you've been wanting"), threats ("If you don't keep this house clean, I'll burn it down"), assaults (later on in this chapter we will look at what constitutes assault), blocking your entrance or exit, and a multitude of other abusive behaviors. This is a very broad definition, as it should be. A broad definition allows a judge to decide whether or not abuse has occurred based on evidence presented. It would be impossible to specify every type of behavior that could be considered assaultive or coercive. However, here is my personal yardstick: if someone makes you feel so uncomfortable that you do something or refrain from doing something against your will, you are probably experiencing some kind of abuse.

Domestic violence is really about power and control. The perpetrator feels the need to control you. If words alone aren't working, the perpetrator's actions escalate until control is reestablished. I will provide examples later in this chapter.

As an attorney, I always ask my clients about any domestic violence in their marriage. I also have them fill out a written questionnaire about possible violence and about how they fight. The questionnaire came about because I needed to find a way to help victims focus on what they've been suffering and open up about it. Many victims of domestic violence deny that they are victims, even when they are asked directly by a divorce lawyer in a law office where they have come to seek counsel about divorce. So I sought the help of counselors who work exclusively with victims of domestic violence who told me that many abuse victims don't even know— except in some back corner of their minds that they are determined to ignore—that what has been going on in their homes qualifies as domestic abuse. What would be really helpful, these counselors told me, is to show them a list of specific actions that constitute violence and ask about these specifically.

The following actions are considered violent intrusions into your personal space. Our legal system considers them to be forms of assault or battery or violence, and many are crimes:

1. shouting/loud voice;
2. name calling;
3. threats of physical harm;
4. threats of perpetrator's suicide (i.e., situations where one spouse threatens to kill himself/herself if the other spouse does a certain thing—leaves, reports abuse to the police, takes the children away, etc.);
5. other kinds of threats (for example, putting something defamatory about the spouse on the Internet, breaking or selling something of great value to the spouse, etc.);
6. blocking exits;
7. spitting;
8. throwing/breaking objects;
9. shoving;
10. hair pulling;
11. grabbing around neck;
12. knocking to ground;
13. hitting, slapping;
14. kicking;
15. displaying a weapon (knife, gun, etc.);
16. forced sexual activity (including such actions as the perpetrator forcing the spouse to watch a porn video or attend a strip club or spouse-swapping club or engage in actions or positions that are uncomfortable, or engage in sex with a third party, or use sex toys or other apparatus that the spouse finds objectionable or painful. It also includes the perpetrator denying sex or loving actions to the spouse as punishment);
17. threaten to kill;
18. attempt to kill.

I must admit that I wouldn't have known to list hair pulling as an act of violence. However, I understand why all these things qualify as a pattern of domestic violence once an expert explained to me that this list contains the first actions a perpetrator may use in controlling his or her spouse. *If a less aggressive action works, the perpetrator does not need to escalate the methods.* So, although name calling and a push into a corner might not physically hurt you, it represents the beginning of a sequence of actions that will escalate until you acquiesce to the perpetrator's demands. Anything your partner does that violates your personal space, restricts your freedom, and/or makes you fear for your safety is domestic violence, and *you should do whatever you have to do to immediately remove yourself from that situation.*

Many people think that an action must physically hurt you or leave a mark before it rises to the level of violence. It doesn't. It is the fear factor rather than the bruise itself that makes the action violent. Again, this is because a lesser action—a threat, a shove, hair pulling—implicitly communicates that previous limits on restraint are no longer in place and worse acts may follow. Many individuals on the receiving end of such treatment feel the real fear *they are intended to feel* but are afraid to report it to the police out of worry they will be dismissed as exaggerating what has been done to them. They become convinced there is too much risk in making that claim; the perpetrator, who has already abandoned civilized restraints on behavior, later may exact revenge. If you are in such a situation, here's what I want you to know: You don't need physical evidence to support your claim of abuse. If you are in fear, you are being abused. Don't worry about "proving" it to someone else; the law-enforcement community now understands a great deal about what constitutes domestic violence, and it's very likely they will take you at your word.

But there's something even more important, and that is for you to come to the clear realization that you are being abused and can do something about it. You don't need a chorus of people behind you validating your claim that your abuser is abusing you. *You* know it, and that is enough to act and get out of there. You don't need a court order to leave your marriage or get yourself to safety.

I can't stress this enough. In my years of practicing family law, I have handled many cases in which there was abuse. I believe the most dangerous situations are those in which the victim is in denial about the degree of danger. When clients tell me they have been abused, I always tell them they need to leave the situation immediately: just go, take the kids out of school, and drive to safety; don't go home for any reason. Sometimes they don't listen. They don't realize how much danger they are in: three of my clients have been murdered by their abusers during the divorce process.

THE BASEMENT PUNISHMENT CASE

Several years ago, a couple came to my office wanting to know if I would mediate their divorce. Nothing happened during their initial consultation to make me suspect domestic violence. As always, I gave them a copy of my domestic violence questionnaire, which is completely confidential and never shared with the spouses. Every potential client must complete this questionnaire before I will work with him or her. Wife filled her own out and sent it back answering no to all the specific questions regarding abuse.

Thank goodness my questionnaire had one last catchall question: "Is there anything else you would like to tell me about your spouse?" The woman wrote in the space provided, "When I am a bad girl, my husband sends me to the basement to sit in a chair and think about what I did wrong."

My "abuse radar" went off. I approached her as a possible victim of abuse. I called her by phone and asked her to tell me what sorts of actions would prompt her husband to call her a "bad girl." After all, she was a fifty-five-year-old woman and didn't have to do everything her husband told her to do; she explained that her husband called her a bad girl for actions as benign as getting dinner on the table ten minutes late. I probed further. She told me he would order her to go to the basement and sit in an old-fashioned wooden school desk for two hours to think about what she had done wrong. She added that he had carved her name in the top of the wooden desk with his hunting knife and hung a noose from a beam in the ceiling directly above so that she could stand on the desk, put the noose around her neck, and easily tip the desk with one foot to hang herself. After two hours of contemplating her "sins," and deciding whether she deserved to live, she could come back upstairs.

This woman was so accustomed to this kind of treatment that she did not see it as abusive. She'd been so brainwashed that she thought she deserved it.

I told her that unfortunately, ethical standards prevented me from mediating a divorce where there is domestic abuse. There is a good reason why mediators should not mediate such cases: if one spouse is intimidated and threatened by the other, how could the mediator trust the abused spouse's agreement on any issue? The perpetrator spouse might be using threats to bring about more favorable terms. Ethical standards also barred me from becoming the private attorney of one spouse who had previously come to me with the other spouse seeking mediation. If a couple comes to my office together seeking mediation services, I can only be their mediator from that point forward; I can never serve in the role of an attorney to represent either of them at any time in the future. Likewise, if an individual seeks my services as an attorney, I can only be that person's attorney from that point forward; I can never serve in the role of a mediator for that person and the spouse in the future.

Because this woman had shared with me that she was being abused, I gave her the name and phone number of an abuse shelter, suggested she call them, and advised her to hire her own private attorney to represent her in the divorce. But the follow-up letter I then wrote to both husband and wife, to officially decline their request to mediate, was very general, so as not to reveal to the husband that I knew about the abuse. I simply wrote that after reading the materials they returned to me, I felt I could not help them come to agreement; they were free to find another mediator or to hire their own private attorneys to proceed with the divorce. I don't know what happened to this couple afterward; I can only hope the wife called the shelter and took steps to remove herself from a dangerous situation.

Victims of domestic violence need a strong advocate to look out for them in a divorce proceeding. Such an advocate should be well versed on the topic of domestic violence, able to decipher whether the victim is giving up any rights just to placate the partner and preempt the partner's wrath. The advocate must help the victim focus on sensibly choosing assets from the marital estate so that she or he will be able to move out of the toxic relationship and establish a new, healthy, independent life. This feat requires emotional and physical support as well as firm legal guidance.

That's why the victim of domestic violence needs to hire an attorney who is well trained in the area of domestic violence or who works in conjunction with a therapist or other professional with a background in assisting domestic violence victims.

ESCAPING ABUSE: BE PROACTIVE

If you are in an abusive marriage, want to escape, and have time on your side, here are some steps to consider:

1. **Secretly inform yourself** of your rights and the choices you have to escape safely.
2. **Open a bank account** at a bank where your spouse does not bank, and put it in your name only, listing your work address or another very safe address, so that statements and other bank mailings never come to the marital residence. When you receive these, do not store them where they could be carried home by mistake.

   Discreetly deposit small, unnoticeable amounts of money whenever you can so that you have enough of an escape fund to cover transportation, a hotel, food, or whatever else you may need over a short period of transition.
3. **Photograph** any marks physical violence has left on you. Go to a hospital emergency room and have a record made. This could be useful later in court.
4. **Add to this list** using suggestions you receive in conversation with your local domestic violence hotline, shelter, or organization.

THE ABUSER WHOSE MOTHER WATCHED HIM ABUSE

I recently helped a friend who was living in an abusive relationship with her husband. This harmful relationship, which was unknown to me while we both lived in the same city, escalated after they moved far away. Her husband's aggressive actions continued in front of his mother, who was visiting, and their young daughter. This did not deter him, not even when his little girl held onto her dad's leg and begged him to "stop hitting Mommy." The perpetrator's mother saw the entire confrontation yet sided with her son. She told my friend that she should change her ways so that she didn't "irritate" her son. When my friend called me for support and advice, I advised her to leave immediately and go to an emergency shelter for abuse victims. I worried that she might not do it. It's a big step, and victims often hesitate because they see it as dangerous, inconvenient, and frightening. It would throw her into unknown territory, as she had never done anything like this before.

Luckily, she followed my advice. She went to a safe place. She got in touch with a local organization for victims of domestic abuse, learned that her situation was far from unique, and listened to solid advice from people who had survived similar situations and who cared about her and her problems. It was then, when she felt safe and supported by others, that she found the courage to go to the hospital for treatment and officially document her injuries. At her request, the hospital took photographs and created a document reporting the incident she described. This document could be a crucial piece of evidence in any legal or law enforcement action she decided to pursue against her husband. While I said earlier that you do not have to wait for physical evidence such as a bruise before leaving and seeking help (since the first and most important thing is to just leave the abusive situation), if you do have abuse-related injuries it is always a good idea to go to a third party, such as a hospital emergency room, to get treatment and documentation of the injuries with photographs if possible.

By this time she was resolved that divorce was the best way forward. I was relieved to hear it, because perpetrators typically will repeat their abusive actions no matter what they promise. Just when I thought she was starting to move ahead on the right track, she told me that she thought she could represent herself in the divorce proceedings. That is a common-enough reaction from someone who is living on a very modest income and is worried about the cost of legal representation. But, as I hastened to tell her, hiring a professional advocate is an absolute necessity in such cases. Victims of domestic violence should never be put in situations where they are negotiating with the perpetrator. Never! It takes time—many months or even years, if it even happens at all, for such victims to heal from the physical and emotional trauma they have experienced. Until then, they usually lack the confidence and resolve to represent themselves effectively, especially when faced with their abusers in a courtroom setting. They are in danger of agreeing to something that is not in their best interests out of a reflexive sense of fear or an ingrained belief that they are not worthy of anything better and could potentially be legally locked into that unfair situation forever. Abuse victims need an experienced legal representative who can advocate for them and help them emerge in the best way possible from the worst chapter of their lives. Ultimately, she hired an attorney who was successful in getting a full order of protection for her and a divorce, wherein she got full custody of their daughter. Dad, of course, got custody time with their daughter, but only under court supervision and after he completed a class on abuse.

Just a note about gender bias in domestic violence: Not all victims are female; many males are abused in marital relationships. We just don't hear much about violence against men. I'm reminded of a male client who came to me seeking an order of protection against his wife, and who ultimately hired me to represent him in the divorce. His wife had attacked him, hitting and slapping him after an argument, while their children were asleep upstairs. He tried to protect himself by pushing her away. Four times in succession she came back at him, slapping and scratching him in the face. Finally, he got to a phone and called 911.

After the police arrived, they wanted to take pictures of the slap marks and scratches on his face and ask him questions about how his wife had attacked him. He felt embarrassed and brushed it off as nothing. He couldn't help thinking that if he were "a real man," he would have been able to stop her. As he told me this story in my office, he hung his head in shame.

I called him by name and looked him directly in the eyes. "The gender of the abuser is not important. It is still abuse. You should be congratulated on your restraint in not returning her violence blow for blow and in picking up the phone to call 911."

His eyes filled with tears. I asked if I could be the person to congratulate him for doing the right thing. He nodded, took a deep breath, and we proceeded to prepare for his order of protection hearing.

There are many theories about why we don't hear more about abuse of men by women, but they are not critical to this chapter. The primary message of this chapter is to warn victims of violent domestic relationships that they need to leave immediately. Unfortunately, it is up to the victims themselves to break the cycle of violence. If they don't leave the situation, their misery will be perpetuated, and their children will suffer as well.

Children in households where parents are locked in an abusive relationship suffer in many ways. The abused parent may be too distracted by pain and fear to provide the love and guidance the child needs. The abusive parent may be so angry and controlling that this colors the relationship with the kids as well. There may be excessive drinking involved, which enables abusive behavior and leads to all sorts of other problems.

Children can grow up feeling that out-of-control situations are normal and home is not a safe place. They can come to believe that adults are powerless to change bad situations. And children also learn from and imitate their parents. If the parents are in a physically violent relationship, children are more likely to make choices in adulthood that model their parents' relationship. They are drawn to what they know. This is the model of love they learned; they may confuse violence or abusive language with intimacy. The longer they witness violence between their parents, the more likely they are to end up in an abusive relationship themselves. Children are just as victimized as the abused parent.

What to do? Whether or not a domestic abuse victim files for divorce, he or she can file a petition called an ex parte order of protection (states may use different terms for this legal action, but the impact is the same). The ex parte order of protection orders the perpetrator to stay away from the victim. The perpetrator cannot phone or make other contact or go to the victim's workplace or home for a specified period of time (usually around ten to fourteen days).

After the specified time has elapsed, the perpetrator can hire legal counsel and plead his or her case to the judge. After a hearing, the judge decides whether or not to issue a full order of protection, which orders the perpetrator to stay away from the victim for a specified period, usually six months to a year, but sometimes longer. Both parties receive copies of the order and so do police stations in the relevant jurisdictions. The order may also be sent over to the criminal court system if there will be criminal prosecution of the perpetrator. Fortunately, court systems now take domestic violence very seriously. In my experience, judges tend to lean toward issuing full orders of protection, since they don't want to risk the victims being violated again.

While the order of protection protects the victim, a common issue that arises is what to do if the couple has young children. If the perpetrator has not harmed the children, should the perpetrator be prevented from seeing his or her children? This is an extremely controversial topic and one that is beyond the scope of this book. However, I will summarize generally so that you have some idea of how such situations might be handled. Procedures differ by jurisdiction, but a common legal response is to arrange custody periods for the children to spend time with the accused parent. To prevent any further escalation between the parents, such custody arrangements involve protected exchanges for the children. This can be achieved by picking a safe, public place for the exchanges and/or arranging for relatives or friends to make the exchanges. The goal is for everyone to be safe and the children to feel as comfortable as possible.

How does an order of protection affect a divorce action? First, it usually eliminates the possibility of joint parenting. If there is so much hostility between Mom and Dad that an order of protection is necessary, then by definition, Mom and Dad probably cannot co-parent. So one parent is given sole physical custody and the other is given intermittent periods of parenting time. In addition, the judge appoints one parent to make important legal decisions concerning the child, such as medical treatment, education, and religious decisions. This means the parents don't have to talk and agree on these important issues. Smaller issues too, such as daily care (bedtime, computer time, daily chores, restrictions on television viewing, etc.) when the child is with a particular parent can be decided by that parent without having to involve the other parent in the decision. So, a full order of protection at the time of divorce can have a significant impact on the parenting plan in that the judge may put one parent in charge of all the major decision making concerning the child.

A full order of protection may influence the judge in another way: ordering that child support and/or maintenance be handled through the court itself as opposed to having one party giving it directly to the other party. This further eliminates the need for contact between the divorcing spouses.

I've heard some lawyers tell their clients that they can "win more in court if they have an order of protection," meaning the judge would likely award more maintenance or more assets to the victim. I don't agree with that statement. Actually, I don't think anyone wins in divorce court. It's not a scenario where one person wins everything in the marital estate and the other loses everything in the marital estate. That just doesn't happen in real life. The majority of the time judges try to achieve an equitable division of the parties' assets and debts without weighing it toward "the good guy" and away from "the bad guy." Now, maybe you're thinking, *What? I thought it used to be that there was always a "good guy" and a "bad guy" in divorce cases!* You're not wrong. For a very long time, in order to get a divorce at all, it was necessary to prove that "your spouse is a louse." You had to prove that your spouse had committed some type of marital misconduct that was listed in the dissolution statute. Then no-fault divorce came along, and the good guy/bad guy scenario was tossed aside. This happened state by state over time. Surprisingly, the very last state to finally allow no-fault divorces was New York, and that happened in 2015. Still, many states have had no-fault divorce for so long that judges by and large have switched over from a punitive approach in dividing marital assets to one that is more evenhanded and based on the actual needs and expenses of each party going forward.

In some states, a judge may look at the parties' behavior during the marriage and decide to give one party a little more out of the marital estate than the other party to make up for dissipation of assets or marital misconduct or grant one spouse a larger share of custody than the other, if the judge finds the behavior of the misbehaving spouse particularly abhorrent. This is at the judge's discretion and it can work to the benefit of, say, a spouse who has been abused. It is also possible that one spouse's suffering at the hands of the other to elicit no sympathy at all from the judge. Again, it depends on your fact situation and the attitude of the judge.

Whether or not you seek court protection, there are choices you can make, now and going forward, to protect yourself and your children. Answering the following questions will help you develop a roadmap for the future.

QUESTIONS

1. Are you living in a marriage with violence and control issues?
2. Do you fear for your safety or the safety of your child?
3. Have you experienced any of the acts of domestic violence listed earlier in this chapter?

If you answered yes to any of the above, you and/or your children are victims of domestic violence and you need to take immediate steps to protect yourself (and perhaps your children) from additional abuse.

If you are hesitant to leave, take an inventory of your concerns:

1. Are you fearful that leaving will make the situation worse?
2. Do you fear you will be alone, with no community of support?
3. Are you thinking you would not be able to support yourself or your children, afford a place to live, finish your education?

If any of these concerns are preventing you from leaving, please know there are organizations waiting to help you at no cost. There are solutions to all these concerns; you simply may not be aware of all your options. A bit of research will serve you very well at this point. If you have even an hour to research your options at a safe place, such as a public library, it will be worth it. Domestic violence websites, for instance, have valuable suggestions that might not occur to you in a crisis situation. Based on the best information you have acquired, start formulating a plan A and plan B.

Having a plan B is important. In this chapter you will find a box with a list of steps you can take now and in the days to come. There is also a box with a list of organizations you can contact for information and help.

Now is the time to identify people and organizations that can help you.

These could include a trustworthy friend, a mentor in another part of your life, a medical practitioner, a member of the clergy (whether or not you belong to that person's congregation).

You might feel terribly alone and powerless right now, but there is a lot of support for you out there. Domestic violence organizations offer concrete assistance as well as many opportunities to find encouragement and hope from others who have successfully rebuilt their lives. These organizations are equipped to find you safe temporary shelter, a long-term safe house, a legal advocate, a therapist, a career counselor; know that you are lucky enough to live in a country that has recognized such needs and provides many options.

It may be hard to take the first step to end the cycle of abuse, but you can do it, because countless others have done it before you. The biggest motivation of all may be your children. You can find the courage for their sakes. You want them to grow up knowing they do not have to be trapped in abusive situations. They will know they can change their lives for the better, because they saw you do it.

INTERNET AND COMPUTER SAFETY

This Information is from the Missouri Coalition against Domestic and Sexual Violence.

I quote it here in full:

> *If you are in danger, please try to use a safer computer that someone abusive does not have direct or remote (hacking) access to.*

Computers can store a lot of private information about what you look at via the Internet, the emails and instant messages you send, Internet-based phone calls you make, web-based purchases and banking, and many other activities. It is not possible to delete or clear all the 'footprints' of your computer or online activities.

It might be safer to use a computer in a public library, at a trusted friend's house, or in an Internet cafe to research an escape plan, new jobs, apartments, bus tickets, or to ask for help.

"If you think your activities are being monitored, they probably are. Abusive people are often controlling and want to know your every move. You don't need to be a computer programmer or have special skills to monitor someone's computer and Internet activities—anyone can do it. There are many ways to monitor computer usage with programs including spyware, keystroke loggers, and hacking tools."

JILL'S STORY: THE LIGHT AT THE END OF THE TUNNEL

I want to share a story about a client who was a victim of domestic violence. She came to me in a wheelchair, crippled in both legs. She had just discovered pornography on her husband's computer and was in a total state of shock. She had three grade school-age daughters of this marriage and was horrified that they might stumble upon the pornography on his computer.

After spending about an hour with her, stories of the horrific abuse she had suffered at the hands of her alcoholic husband came out. Yet, it seemed she was seeking a divorce more to protect her daughters from pornography than herself from abuse. She told me stories of her husband beating her with her own cane; chasing her down the hallway while she tried to go as fast as she could in her wheelchair to get away from him; depriving her of money to buy food and necessities for herself and the children; calling her derogatory names; and making fun of her in front of the children. Fortunately, we were able to settle her case rather quickly without going to trial.

I have to tell you more about this client so you can really appreciate her story. She was and is one of the kindest, most forgiving, generous, loving, and selfless women I know. Her escape from abuse began with mountains of fear, insecurity, and worry about how she was going to support herself and three children. She exited my life after the divorce was final, as do most of my clients. However, she called me one day several years later to see if I would have lunch with her at a restaurant near my office. This was a first for me, but I gladly agreed. I was looking for her wheelchair when I entered the restaurant. Instead, I saw her standing on her own two legs, which was only possible because she was brave enough to suffer through numerous operations. She was also half the size I remembered, as she had lost about 240 pounds so she could stand on her own legs again. Her children were thriving in school; she had a job, and her face glowed with love and compassion for life as she told me the story of her transformation.

She had no bitterness toward her husband as well as no regrets about the divorce. She saw life as a joyous opportunity to live in peace with all things. Heck, she was doing better than I was! I could not believe her transformation. And she credited *me* for all the changes in her life! I was in awe. Wait—it gets better. She later started her own thriving business, which she continues to enjoy at the time of the writing of this book. She ultimately built her business into a thriving million-dollar empire and now helps other victims of abuse. She has established a level of living beyond most people's dreams and generously shares her wealth and time with family, friends, and her community.

If you are currently a victim of abuse, but afraid to move out of that relationship, I hope you remember this story and realize what can be waiting for you at the other end of the dark tunnel you are now in if you will just keep trudging through it!

NATIONAL DOMESTIC VIOLENCE ORGANIZATIONS

National Domestic Violence Hotline, www.ndvh.org.
National Stalking Resource Center, www.ncvc.org/src.
National Clearinghouse for the Defense of Battered Women, www.ncdbw.org/.
National Network to End Domestic Violence, http://nnedv.org.
Domestic Shelters, www.domesticshelters.org.
Sojourner Center, www.sojurnercenter.org.

DON'T DO THIS

Abuse victims often make a huge mistake at the hearing to decide if they can get a full order of protection. It's something they do when they get on the stand and answer questions about what their spouse did to them and why they are still afraid, and it undermines the strength of their case.

The mistake is to act stronger than you are.

This has happened in my practice enough times that I feel it is important to mention here. Domestic violence victims have told me that when they finally get to tell their story in court, they feel angrier and braver than they have ever felt before. They are separated from their abuser by a judge, two attorneys, a bailiff and lots of people watching. Consequently, they can take on an unusual air of arrogance and power they usually cannot summon. This can make the judge think that they are not afraid or intimidated by their abuser.

This feeling of power is only temporary, but the judge doesn't know that. I have seen some judges deny the full order of protection because they think the victim is not really afraid. Don't let this happen to you.

HOW TO SAVE YOURSELF, YOUR MONEY, AND YOUR CHILDREN DURING DIVORCE

After reading the previous chapters, you have gotten answers to many of your questions about divorce. But the most important questions I hope I've answered is how to save yourself, your money, and your children during divorce. Let's start by recalling why you are considering divorce in the first place. Remember the list of rights I posed to you in the very first chapter?

You have the right to

- be happy;
- lead a fulfilling and peaceful life, free of conflict;
- be the creator of your future;
- live free of fear for your physical safety;
- live free of constant worry about the stability of your family;
- exercise your power to protect yourself from abuse;
- be respected by yourself and the other significant people in your life;

- live an abundant life with the ability to make your own choices about money; and
- live in a place where you are safe and content. You deserve your own sanctuary.

If you believe you deserve the rights listed above, and after giving this a lot of consideration, you still think divorcing your spouse will lead you toward this better life, then it's time to take some action.

The following are the action steps I would recommend.

- **SAVE YOURSELF**

  - Choose which method of divorce best fits you and your spouse. If at all possible, choose mediation because it can save whatever relationship you still have with your spouse, save you lots of money, and most importantly, save your children from the devastating effects of your conflict with your spouse during divorce.
  - Pick your lawyer. You want one that specializes in family law and has lots of experience. Read his or her website carefully, because you can learn a lot about a lawyer by looking at what he or she thinks is important enough to put on the website.
  - Ask your lawyer whether you need a legal proceeding called a pendente lite. This is an emergency hearing where the judge can give you temporary exclusive possession of your home, car, and bank accounts, and assign a parenting arrangement for your children to see you and your spouse in a predictable schedule.
  - I also strongly recommend getting a counselor with whom you are comfortable and feel can be supportive through this process. Remember, you are going to be dealing with some strong emotions that you may not usually encounter in your daily life. A counselor can help you wind your way

through the five stages of grief people feel during divorce. It is similar to the five stages of grief people experience during the death of a spouse or loved one. (Divorce can be even worse than death because you still have to see your former spouse and possibly make decisions with him or her in the future while still trying to detach from that person.) It might be helpful for you to investigate the five stages of death by Elizabeth Kübler Ross. She explains the grieving process in her 1969 book, *On Death and Dying.* The five stages are denial, anger, bargaining, depression, and acceptance. The problem is that you don't go through these stages in a linear timeline and then you are finished grieving. Instead, you may skip around and go back to previous stages before you get to the end of your process. But to be happy after divorce, I believe it is critical for you to pass through these stages.

- Don't lie to your lawyer. It can cost you your case as well as a lot of money. I realize divorce lawyers usually see people at the worst time in their lives, when they are feeling angry, bitter, crushed, jealous, or guilty. People will lie when they are caught up in feelings like this. Since that is what we see all the time as divorce lawyers, it becomes difficult for us to know how the world outside of marital crisis compares in terms of general behavior and outlook on life. I am always struck by the clients—and lawyers—who lie with impunity, with the full expectation that their lies will be believed no matter how absurd or easy to puncture. Maybe what I am seeing now is not necessarily more people who lie, but more people who are willing to take the gamble that lying will pay off. Lying is a very risky business, especially in legal proceedings. The danger in getting caught is higher than ever and the penalties can be severe. What I hope you see is that lying is, indeed, a gamble that's just not worth taking. Gambling is wishful thinking that flies in the face of logic and common sense. It seldom pays off.

- **SAVE YOUR MONEY**

  - You can ask the judge to make your spouse give you money for temporary child support, maintenance, and legal fees while also protecting (freezing) other assets so your spouse cannot deplete them. Your lawyer can give you specific directions on how to proceed.

  - Another thing that you can do to save your money is *do everything your lawyer tells you to do in a timely manner.* In the legal system, time is money. Every time you call your lawyer, it costs money. Every time your lawyer calls or emails you asking for you to send documents that have already been requested but have not yet been sent by you, it costs you money. By providing all the information your lawyer asks for when he or she asks for it, you save your money.

  - Don't call your lawyer every time a question pops into your mind. Instead, write it down on a piece of paper, wait until you have ten questions, and then schedule a phone consult with your lawyer at a specific time. This prevents you from playing phone tag with your lawyer, which is frustrating and expensive.

  - Tell your lawyer your entire story. Remember the puzzle pieces in the box? If you leave some puzzle pieces out, your lawyer will not have all the pieces he or she needs to help you create the future you want.

  - Make certain the assets you're taking are the ones most important to creating the future you want. You need to get crystal clear about what you need to take with you from the marital pot of assets to help create your future.

THE MOTORCYCLE MAMA

Once I was mediating with a couple where the husband was the main breadwinner and the wife stayed at home to raise the children.

The youngest child was now in high school; Mom could work but just didn't have any specialized skills or experience. I asked her what she would like to do if the sky was the limit.

She answered, "Be a cosmetologist."

"Great," I replied. "Then you need to check out which cosmetology schools or programs are the best, how long their program is, and how much it costs. Bring that information back to your next mediation session." (She also drew a picture of her "perfect future" where she owned her own beauty shop and had a long line of customers. That shows vision and purpose.)

At the next mediation session, we focused on dividing assets. One asset in the marital pot to be divided was a Harley Davidson motorcycle, worth approximately $10,000. Wife said she wanted that asset.

"Have you ever driven a motorcycle before?" I asked.

"No," she answered.

I questioned again, "Do you have a license to drive a motorcycle?"

"No," she answered sharply.

Then I asked, "Do you like to collect motorcycles?"

Again, she replied, "No."

I got to the final question: "How is taking this motorcycle from the marital pot going to help you to accomplish your dreams of owning your own beauty shop?"

She said, "It isn't. But I just don't want my husband to get it. You see, that motorcycle plays a big role in *why* we are getting divorced. If my husband had spent as much time with me as he did working on his motorcycle, we probably would not be getting divorced right now. So there is no way I am going to let him take the motorcycle that broke up our marriage!"

Her anger and resentment over that Harley was probably well deserved. But I asked her another question that put her back on the right track. "If your goal is to start your own beauty business, you need cash to do that, right?" She agreed. "You don't need a motorcycle, do you?"

"No," she replied. "But you don't understand how mad I am about that damn motorcycle."

"Did you put a motorcycle in your 'perfect picture' of your future? I don't see one in your drawing. What I see is the need for cash—to go to school and learn a new skill, to support you until you learn this new skill, and to open your own business, not a Harley in your driveway."

That revelation met with the sound of crickets for a few minutes. Finally, she reluctantly agreed. Husband could take the Harley in exchange for $10,000 cash. I asked him if that was what he wanted to do and he quickly agreed.

By focusing on the blueprint for the future they wanted instead of punishing for the past, this couple continued to make good decisions for their life *after* divorce. And that's what it is all about: creating a better future, not punishing for the past. If wife would have thought it through a little longer, she would have realized that if she demanded taking the Harley, husband would have just cashed in something and bought himself a bigger, better, badder new motorcycle anyway. So she still would not be punishing him. Rather, she would be giving him an excuse to buy another motorcycle and blame her for it.

Trying to take all the assets your spouse wants doesn't really hurt them. Living the best and most rewarding life you can live after divorce is really the best revenge anyway!

• FINALLY, BUT MOST IMPORTANT OF ALL, SAVE YOUR CHILDREN

- Remember, conflict is poison to your children. If you and your spouse are fighting, then your children are in danger, and only you can save them. How? Remove them from the conflict.

    I.   Do not argue in front of them.

II.   Do not disparage your spouse in front of them.

III. Do not try to get them on your side.

IV.   Do not use them as your confidant to cry on their shoulder.

V.   Do not ask them to be your messengers.

VI.   Do not ask them to keep secrets for you.

VII. Allow them to set boundaries to protect themselves from the conflict and then honor those boundaries.

VIII. Get them into counseling if they want to talk to someone.

- Use mediation as your process of divorce if possible. The mediator will help you create a plan that protects your children and encourage you to follow methods to keep them out of your conflict, as laid out in the section above.

- Remember that your children may experience collateral damage after the divorce is over. Their feelings and fears about your divorce can resurrect during their dating years with no advance notice. If you remain aware of this danger and watch them closely during their teens and early twenties, you can help them seek assistance and understanding of what is happening to them. If they exhibit signs of collateral damage:

    1. Remember that you are the adults in this situation. It is your job as parents to protect your children and give them power to express their needs and boundaries. When you are in the midst of a torrid divorce, it's tempting to only think of your pain and suffering. But your children are suffering also; they just may be doing it in silence. Remember this and get them the support they need.

    2. Finally, remember: *You are their best guardians.*

Printed in the United States
By Bookmasters